IDEAS ON TRIAL

CHARLES DREW

PIONEER OF BLOOD PLASMA

Linda Trice

McGraw-Hill

New York St. Louis San Francisco Auckland Bogotá Caracas
Lisbon London Madrid Mexico City Milan Montreal
New Delhi San Juan Singapore Sydney Tokyo Toronto

A Bank Street Biography

Ideas on Trial

The *Ideas on Trial* series presents dramatic stories of men and women in science and medicine who waged heroic struggles and risked their comfort, freedom, reputations, and sometimes their lives, for the sake of pursuing their work.

The authors use a docu-drama, "you are there" style to tell these exciting stories. Wherever possible, actual reported scenes and dialog are used, along with quotes from letters, diaries, newspapers, and journals of the time. In a few cases, however, the authors had to invent scenes and dialog for events that did occur, but for which there was no reported scene or dialog.

Library of Congress Cataloging-in-Publication Data
Trice, Linda.
    Charles Drew : pioneer of blood plasma / Linda Trice.
        p. cm.—(Ideas on trial)
    Summary: A biography of the black surgeon who conducted research on the properties and preservation of blood plasma and was a leader in establishing blood banks.
    ISBN 0-07-135317-8
    1. Drew, Charles Richard, 1904–1950—Juvenile literature. 2. Surgeons—United States—Biography—Juvenile literature. 3. Afro-American surgeons—United States—Biography—Juvenile literature. 4. Blood banks—United States—Biography—Juvenile literature. [1. Drew, Charles Richard, 1904–1950. 2. Physicians. 3. Afro-Americans—Biography. 4. Blood.] I. Title. II. Series.

RD27.35.D74 T755 2000
617'.092—dc21
[B]   00-026137

1 2 3 4 5 6 7 8 9 0 DOC/DOC 0 9 8 7 6 5 4 3 2 1 0

ISBN 0-07-135317-8

The Bank Street Series Project Editor was Elisabeth Jakab.

The sponsoring editor for this book was Griffin Hansbury, the developmental editor was Mary Loebig Giles, the editing supervisor was Jane Palmieri, and the production supervisor was Charles H. Annis. The cover and text were designed and set in New Century Schoolbook by Marsha Cohen/ Parallelogram Graphics.

McGraw-Hill books are available at special quantity discounts to use as premiums and sales promotions, or for use in corporate training programs. For more information, please write to the Director of Special Sales, McGraw-Hill, Two Penn Plaza, New York, NY 10121-2298.

To my parents, Charles and Harriet Trice, who told me about Dr. Charles Drew when I was a little girl

The author thanks the people who helped with this book, especially: Ann Bases; Len Bases, MD; Pamela Burch; Vashti R. Curlin, MD; Amy Elder; Conrad Harper, Esq.; LaSalle Lefall, MD; Jane Marshall; Walter Dean Myers; Kaaryn Nailor; Debbie Trice; Dorothy Trice, MD; Sally Wecksler; Michael Winston, Ph.D.

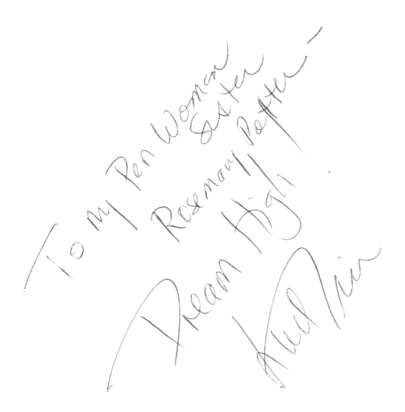

CONTENTS

1

THE DOOMSDAY FLU

The sound came again. Fifteen-year-old Charles Drew stood outside his sister Elsie's bedroom door, rigid with concern. Again she coughed, then she softly moaned.

It was a hot summer, like every summer in Washington, D.C., that young Charlie Drew could remember. Surely the intense heat was making his little sister uncomfortable.

Thirteen-year-old Elsie Drew had tuberculosis, (TB). In July 1919, there was no cure for TB.

Charlie walked across the second-floor landing and stopped at the sound of his parents' voices. It was Sunday and they were getting dressed for church. Charlie didn't mean to eavesdrop, but he couldn't help it. He heard his mother say, "Elsie's getting worse, not better, Richard. I don't know what we should do."

"Let's just pray that she doesn't get this Spanish Flu that's going around. With her weakened condition she'd never survive." There was a pause; then Charlie heard, "Nora, our little Elsie may die."

, Die? Surely they couldn't mean it! There had to be something that could be done. But what?

He was the eldest and felt responsible for his younger brother and sisters. He always would.

He walked into his little sister's bedroom. She was still asleep, her soft brown curls spread out against the crisp white pillowcase.

Charlie wanted to help Elsie. He wanted her to get better. But what could he do? He didn't know. There had to be something. She couldn't die. Charlie wouldn't let her die. His eyes filled with tears.

He ran down the stairs to the parlor where his best friend Montague Cobb waited. Monty had spent the night with the Drews.

The young men went outside and sat on the porch steps. It wasn't yet noon, but the sun was intense. Their plaid knickers scratched their summer-tanned legs.

Monty waved his hand in front of his face, trying to fan a breeze. Elsie's coughing had kept him awake most of last night. Monty remembered his parents' prediction that Elsie would probably never see another Christmas. Trying to get Charlie's mind off his concern about Elsie, he asked, "Is your grandmother a good cook?"

"The best. Wait until you taste her pound cake. Maybe she'll make it for dessert."

The Drews always had Sunday dinner with Charlie's grandparents after they attended the Nineteenth Street

Baptist Church. Mrs. Drew was a deaconess, and Mr. Drew and the children sang in the choir.

Just then the city morgue's van drove slowly down the street. "Let's go see where they're going," Charlie said.

The boys ran after the van. A few blocks later, it pulled into a circular driveway. The two men who got out wore black suits, dark ties, and black hats. Their noses and mouths were covered by white masks made of gauze with side straps that fastened over the men's ears.

"That's the Bayer's house," Charlie told Monty as they approached. "Mr. Bayer owns the bank on Connecticut Avenue."

"How do you know that?" Monty asked.

"My dad laid the carpet when they moved in. He took me along one day." Charlie paused as he remembered the interior of the house. "When you first go in, there is a chandelier in the foyer and mirrors so tall you can see your whole body."

"If their house is so fancy, I'll bet they have a piano," Monty said. "All of our friends have pianos."

"Not like this piano," Charlie said. The piano in the Drew home was a simple upright.

"Is it like the Cook's piano?" One of their friends, Mercer Cook, was the son of famous musicians. Mercer's grandfather was the Dean of the Howard University School of Law.

Charlie didn't know the piano Monty was talking about, but he said, "The Bayers have a grand piano with a real silk shawl draped over it. The whole house has expensive things in it. It's almost as magnificent as the house of the President of Howard University!"

The men had left the front door open. The boys moved forward to peer inside. "See," Charlie said. "I told you."

The chandelier in the foyer was grand indeed. The midday sunlight sparkled off the crystals. The mirrors on either side caught the sunlight and filled the tiny entryway with light.

"It's the flu," Charlie heard one of the men say. "Look at the bodies. They have brown spots over the cheek bones. With some people it spreads all over and you can't tell if the deceased was colored or white."

"I first saw it in Fort Riley, back in Kansas," the shorter man said. "In March of 1918. I'll never forget it. We had five hundred soldiers down with it within a week. Then I was in Camp Devens, Massachusetts. About one hundred died a day. There weren't enough coffins. We had to let the bodies freeze and then stacked them up, like cordwood."

Fascinated, the boys hurried quietly in. They stood in the hall just outside the parlor, out of view of the men.

A faint stench filled the house.

Huge wilted palm trees in pots looked as if they hadn't been watered in weeks. In front of the trees was a red velvet loveseat. The two men were facing it as they spoke to one another, their backs to the boys. Charlie could tell that one of the bodies on the loveseat was a woman in a pink satin dress. The other was a man wearing navy blue trousers.

"Husband and wife, I'll bet," one of the men said rubbing his forehead. The other unfurled the morgue stretcher. "Let's get on with this."

Charlie held a finger up to his lips and motioned Monty to follow him.

They tiptoed down the hall. In the kitchen they saw dirty dishes stacked up in the sink. The plates on the long wooden table held moldy and half-eaten food that looked as if it had been sitting there for more than a week. Flies were clustered around something on one of the plates. Charlie couldn't tell what it was. He turned his head away when he saw maggots oozing out. The servants must have left a long time ago. "How long do you think they've been dead?" he whispered.

Monty worked in a pharmacy after school. He should know. "A week maybe," he whispered authoritatively. "Some people call it the Three Day Flu because they die in three days, but other people seem to die within a day. Their lungs fill up and they drown in their own blood."

Charlie's eyebrows shot up. He was impressed by his friend's knowledge. "Let's look at the bodies!"

They hid behind the pantry door and listened to the men talking. Finally, they heard the men carrying one of the bodies out of the house.

The boys hurried down the hallway into the parlor. A man's body lay on the sofa. It must have been Mr. Bayer, but Charlie couldn't recognize the face. It had rotted away.

The smell of the decaying corpse was terrible. Charlie turned his head and hoped he wouldn't throw up.

A New York street cleaner wearing a mask to check the spread of the influenza epidemic c. 1919. (Corbis-Bettmann.)

When they heard the men coming back inside, the boys dashed into the dining room, then back to the hall. From there they made their escape out to the sidewalk.

"What a terrible way to die," Charlie said.

"Now I understand why they closed the schools and the churches last year," Monty said.

"Out of the way, boys." The men came out carrying a stretcher covered with a black cloth.

They put the corpse in the back of the van.

"You boys shouldn't be playing around here," the tall man said. "You should go on home and get down on your knees and thank God that you've been spared from this Doomsday Flu."

"Let's go!" The short man had gotten into the van and was sitting behind the driver's seat.

"What about the baby?" Charlie grabbed the tall man's arm. "You can't go. Where's the baby? They have a little girl. I think her name is Lucinda."

"We didn't see a baby." The man called to the driver, "We'd better go back and look. She might still be alive."

As Charlie and Monty waited on the sidewalk, three little girls skipped along the street singing a grim ditty that was popular throughout the country:

"I had a little bird,
And its name was Enza.
I opened up the window,
And in-flu-enza."

Charlie winced, thinking first of little Lucinda Bayer, then of his sister.

When the men came back out, the tall one had a bundle in his arms. It was the baby girl. Her arm hung limply over the man's hand.

The Doomsday Flu

More people died during the Spanish Flu, as it was called, than were killed in World War I. It was called a "pandemic" because it was a worldwide epidemic. It was so deadly that it killed more people than the feared Black Plague of Europe's Middle Ages. Some people called it the Doomsday Flu.

Between 20 and 40 million people died worldwide, 675,000 of them Americans, more than ten times as many as were killed in action. Forty-three thousand American soldiers who fought in Europe died from the flu.

Even now, no one knows exactly what caused the flu or why so many people died.

In 1998, a scientific expedition went to Norway's Spitzbergen Island to take tissue samples from the buried, frozen bodies of people who died of the Doomsday Flu. The scientists did not dig up the bodies, they dug down to them, took tissue samples, then covered them back up. The scientists felt that analyzing these samples might help them to understand and more effectively fight new flu strains as well as other diseases.

Charlie rushed to the man's side. "Is she all right? Does she have the flu?"

"Probably not," the man said. The child's eyes were

Researchers in protective clothing prepare to take tissue samples from the graves of six coal miners who were killed by the Spanish Flu over 80 years ago, Spitzbergen, Norway, August 1998. (AP / Wide World Photos.)

closed and Charlie couldn't tell if she was still breathing. Her lace-trimmed dress was covered with grime and her mother's blood. "If she had the flu, she would be dead by now. The child is just starving and dehydrated. With her parents dead and the servants gone, there was no one to feed her. Another day and she'd be dead."

Charlie and Monty stood on the sidewalk long after the van pulled away. What they had seen and heard was upsetting.

Charlie's eyes filled with tears as he thought of Elsie. "Little children should not have to die."

"They told us in school about vaccines for smallpox and so many of the other diseases that used to kill people," Monty said. "But it isn't enough. More needs to be done. People shouldn't die like this."

"Maybe you could do something about it," Monty suggested.

"What can I do? I'm only fifteen years old!"

"You're a good student. Maybe you could become a doctor or something?"

"No. You know that I'm going to be an engineer when I grow up, and build canals and bridges."

"Well, if you were a doctor, maybe you could find a cure for children like little Lucinda."

"My father doesn't have that kind of money. He's a carpet layer. My mother trained to be a schoolteacher, but she doesn't work. We don't even live in our own house. We have always lived with my grandparents. How could I ever become a doctor, Monty?"

But as he and Monty walked back to the Drew home, Charlie thought about Monty's idea. Could he really become a doctor?

2

THE RED SUMMER OF 1919

The first sound Charlie heard when he and Monty returned to the Drew house was his sister coughing. If rich people like the Bayers died from the flu, what chance did Elsie have? Why couldn't doctors cure all the children who got sick?

The boys walked back to the kitchen where Richard Drew was washing the breakfast dishes. "I don't think I want to be an engineer when I grow up," Charlie told his father. "I think I want to be a doctor. I need to find a way to keep people from getting sick, to keep people from dying."

"Me, too," said Monty.

Richard Drew grinned, proud of his ambitious son and his friend. The three sat down at the table. "Things are getting better for our folks, boys. Soon people will realize that we're all the same. They will stop this non-

*Charlie and his siblings. Elsie is seated. (Charles Drew Papers /
Moorland-Spingarn Research Center, Howard University.)*

sensical talk that Negroes are inferior. Just look at what our boys did over in Europe during the war. Negro soldiers won the top medals for bravery." The boys had heard about this many times. Even their teachers at school talked about it.

"I'm sure racism will end soon, and all colleges and medical schools will admit Negro students," Richard Drew said. "You boys are on the right path. Keep studying and do well in school, and I'm sure you both will become doctors."

Suddenly there was a knock on the door.

It was Mr. Mancini from their former neighborhood. Charlie noticed that the man looked worried.

"Richard, I need to talk to you," he said quietly. "We'd better sit out on the porch. I don't want Mrs. Drew and the younger children to hear this."

The two men sat in wicker rockers, the boys on the steps.

"What's wrong?" Richard Drew asked.

"I know your family usually goes to church on Sundays," Mr. Mancini said. "Maybe it would be best if you all stayed home today. Last night a crowd of white people stormed into the southwest part of the city. They beat every Negro they saw. I saw them pull a colored woman off a streetcar. They beat her to death. I wanted to help her. I really did. But there were so many of them." He paused to wipe away the tears in his eyes. "Two of my cousin's friends were in the mob, wearing their uniforms. One is a sailor, the other a soldier. There

The Great War and Racism

World War I, which took place between 1914 and 1918, was called "The Great War." For the first time in history just about every nation in Europe went to war. The United States entered the war in 1917. Thousands of African-American soldiers in the U.S. Army fought bravely; many were awarded France's top medal, the Croix de Guerre. When they returned to the United States, they naturally expected an end to segregation. They would be disappointed. They had been allowed to fight and die for their country, but in many places, especially in the South, they were kept from voting or even sitting down to eat in restaurants.

was even a woman in the mob from my church." He shook his head, still bewildered by the sudden madness of people he counted as friends and acquaintances. "It's rumored that it's still going on. I have no idea when it will end."

"It's been going on for years," Richard Drew said frowning. "But this summer is the worst. I heard that mobs burnt Negro-owned businesses in Tulsa, Oklahoma." He shook his head sadly. "They chased all the colored people out of Forsythe County, Georgia, and burned Rosewood, Florida, to the ground. They are lynching people in the country and burning down homes and businesses in towns and cities all over America. Who knows when it will end? Who knows how long it will last?"

"But this is the nation's capital!" Mr. Mancini cried. "How can it happen here?"

After Mr. Mancini left, Richard Drew went inside to tell his wife they would not be going to church that morning. They wouldn't be going out for Sunday dinner either. Monty wouldn't get a chance to sample that pound cake.

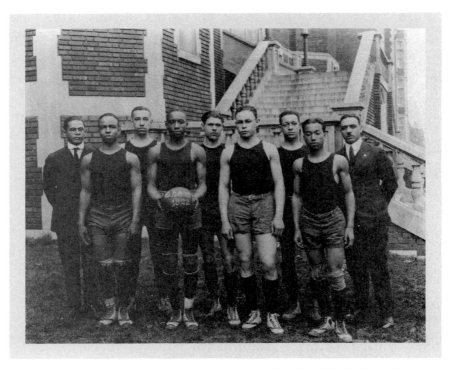

Charles Drew (fourth from right) with the Dunbar High School basketball team, 1922. (Charles Drew Papers / Moorland-Spingarn Research Center, Howard University.)

The Red Summer of 1919

Shortly after African-American soldiers returned home from World War I, some white Americans, prodded by white supremacist organizations like the Ku Klux Klan, increased their physical harassment of blacks even to the extent of lynching African-American soldiers wearing the uniform of the U.S. Army. Many white bigots were furious that blacks had been allowed to fight in World War I and that Europeans had treated them as equals.

The violence reached its height during 1919. That year, between April and October, armed whites attacked 26 black communities throughout the United States, prompting historians to call that period the "Red Summer." In Washington, D.C., in July, attacks on blacks raged for three days. Three hundred people were killed or wounded. The violence ended when African-Americans fought back with guns.

Charlie clutched an old baseball. But as much as he loved sports, he just wasn't in the mood. Monty wasn't either. Neither said a word.

Richard Drew came back out to the porch and sat down. After a few moments he said, "Charlie. Monty. The murders of our people are terrible, but don't let that keep you from your dreams. 'Excellence of performance can overcome racial bias,'" he said, using the words which were to become Charlie Drew's motto throughout

Violence against blacks was hardly news. Between 1898 and 1943, white mobs, often helped by white policemen, attacked black communities. In rural areas, thousands of black men, women, and children were beaten, lynched, or burned alive. In towns and cities, armed whites burned black churches, schools, and homes.

In 1909, the NAACP (the National Association for the Advancement of Colored People) was created by black and white Americans. In 1919, it and other organizations protested against the "Red Summer" attacks, proposed antilynching laws, brought legal action, and through reports and publicity won the sympathy of a shocked public. Currently the NAACP is the largest civil rights group in the United States that fights against the oppression of minorities.

his life, the motto he learned at Nineteenth Street Baptist Church and at Dunbar High School. "We need bright young people to stand up to racists the way our soldiers stood up to the enemy in the war. It's up to you young people to change the world."

"How?" Charlie asked.

"If you're going to get anywhere in this life, the road you have to take is a little highway called Education."

Charlie knew he shouldn't remind his father that

he'd heard him say the same thing over a hundred times.

Richard Drew looked over at Monty. "I expect all five of my children to go to college, even Charlie's three sisters."

Charlie thought of his sister Elsie. She would never get to college if the doctors couldn't cure her.

He thought of little Lucinda Bayer, who had been hours from death when the men from the morgue rescued her. "Dad, I think I want to be a doctor. I need to find a way to keep people from dying."

"First, you have to graduate from college. Then if your grades are good, really good, you might get accepted into the medical school at Howard University here in Washington, D.C., or Meharry Medical College down in Nashville, Tennessee. They both accept Negro students." Richard Drew reminded him, "Medical school is expensive. It costs as much as college."

"I'll never be able to save up that much money."

"No one said it was going to be easy. You and your brother sell newspapers downtown. You've worked on construction sites. Last summer your teacher got you that job in the glass factory in New Jersey. You can do it," he said putting his hand on his son's shoulder. "I know you can. Lots of people work and go to school at the same time." He smiled at Charlie. "Son, we'll find a way."

3

FRIENDS FOR LIFE

Charlie Drew, now an Amherst College junior, pulled down his sweater. He was very proud of the big letter "A" stitched on the front. He earned letters in sports at Amherst just as he had back in high school. He was so good in track that he was the only freshman to earn a letter. Now he was captain of the track team and the football team's star player.

"Hey, Charlie. Catch."

Drew spun around, jumped in the air, and caught the football. "Nice throw, Monty!"

Monty Cobb ran up, laughing. "We can't get anything by you."

"We tried," Bill Hastie said. The three young men and a fourth, Mercer Cook, had been best friends in high school. The four would remain good friends throughout life. As one Amherst schoolmate remembered them, the four had such a close bond that they "almost moved as one."

It was a sunny Friday afternoon in September 1925 in Amherst, Massachusetts. A brisk wind whipped red leaves around Charlie's ankles as he and his friends ran across the college's lawn, tossing the hard leather football back and forth between them.

Charlie had a partial scholarship. His family sent him some money, and waiting tables gave him the rest that he needed.

The young men raced each other to a waiting bus. Charlie won, as usual.

His teammates cheered as he mounted the stairs. They knew he would lead them to victory in the football game against Princeton.

Monty sat next to Charlie as the bus pulled out of the campus. "I don't know if you've heard about Princeton."

Charlie grinned with confidence. "Monty, Amherst can beat any school. Amherst is the best."

"Princeton has a bad reputation as far as Negroes are concerned." Monty lowered his voice even more. "Before the Civil War, it was a favorite school for the sons of rich southern plantation owners. Some of them still seem to have a plantation mentality. They think that they can scare colored players out of a win. I've heard that they'll call us names and maybe even throw things at us during the game."

"Don't worry. I can handle it," Charlie said. "If we stoop to their level, we'll lose for sure. We were raised to be gentlemen, not ruffians. I'm just going to play my

Charles Drew as a member of the Amherst football team.
(Charles Drew Papers/Moorland-Spingarn Research
Center, Howard University.)

best game out there." Charlie's smile hid the plan that was taking shape in his mind. "Maybe I'll give them a taste of what colored men are up to these days."

Traveling with the team was part of the fun of playing college sports. There was always the sense of anticipation as the train rattled its way to a different city.

The team arrived at Trenton, New Jersey, late Friday night, and the players helped the equipment manager unload their gear. After a short ride from Trenton's train station, the team checked into the Stacy-Trent, the hotel that Princeton's athletic department had recommended.

Players were assigned rooms, then dropped off their gear before having a team dinner. Coach McLaughry reminded them that the game against Princeton was going to be rough and that a good night's sleep would be an excellent idea.

But that night Charlie barely slept at all. Phone calls kept coming through the switchboard, asking for him by name. When Charlie answered the phone, he heard racial slurs and threats. Sometimes the callers would pretend to be fans of his, only to end their conversations by telling him what kind of accident they hoped would happen to him on the football field. Even after he stopped picking up the phone, it rang until early Saturday morning.

Game day.

The atmosphere at Princeton was what Charlie had always hoped it would be. The stands were filled with

Princeton rooters, many of them waving pennants emblazoned with the Princeton tiger. Cheerleaders did cartwheels on the sidelines, and the Princeton band blared a brassy tune.

But some Princeton supporters tried to ruin what was looking like an otherwise perfect day. They shouted ugly words at the black players as the Amherst team came through the gates.

The teams warmed up in the bright sunshine. A few of the Princeton players came over and said hello. One of them asked which of the Amherst players was Drew, and he was pointed out. The Princeton player looked at Charlie and nodded. Good, Charlie thought to himself, they had heard about him.

In 1925 all the members of football teams played both offense and defense. On offense, Charlie played in the backfield and carried the ball on running plays. On defense, he played linebacker. It would be his job to stop the Princeton running backs if they got past the line of scrimmage.

When Amherst went on the defensive, a Princeton player called out a racial slur and added, "We're going to run right over you Drew!"

Charlie smiled confidently. Some of the callers the night before had said the same thing. Maybe the Princeton players actually believed it.

The ball was snapped into play, and Princeton made a run toward the center of the line, which the Amherst line stopped after a short gain. The Amherst tackle

Friends for Life

Charles Drew's friends from Dunbar High School and Amherst College, Monty Cobb, Bill Hastie, and Mercer Cook, all obtained advanced degrees, and like Drew worked to end racism.

W. MONTAGUE COBB, MD, a Professor at Howard University's College of Medicine, taught anatomy to almost half of America's black doctors. He helped integrate America's hospitals, public and private, and promoted his theory that the poor health of blacks was not genetic as many whites believed, but was caused by poverty and racism, a theory many people agree with today.

WILLIAM HASTIE graduated with honors from Harvard Law School, was Dean of Howard University's School of Law from 1939 to 1946, became the first black governor (when he was appointed to rule the American territory the Virgin Islands from 1946 to 1949), and was

slapped his hands together, pleased with the way the line had held fast against the Princeton run. But Charlie noticed that it hadn't been Jake Slagle, the hard-hitting back, who had carried the ball. Princeton was just testing to see how good Amherst was.

The next play saw the Princeton tackles and guards cross block and pick up six hard yards. It was third and a yard to go for a Princeton first down.

the first black judge of the U.S. Court of Appeals (1949–1971). As a lawyer, he brought suits that helped end racial discrimination. In the 1940s he and Drew worked to end racism in America's Armed Forces through interviews, speeches, and contacting influential friends. He was appointed civilian aide to Secretary of War Henry L. Stimson, at the time the highest government office held by an African-American. When his attempts to end violence and discrimination against black soldiers were ignored, he resigned in protest.

W. MERCER COOK earned a Ph.D. from Brown (1936) and served as Ambassador to the West African nations of Niger (1961–1964) and Senegal (1964–1966). A noted scholar of French and African literature, he taught at Howard University and Atlanta University and, through his writings, introduced the world to black authors from such French-speaking countries as Haiti and Senegal.

"Okay, guys, let's dig in and stop them here!" the Amherst left guard said.

Charlie was playing left outside linebacker and was ready to move in to stop an off-tackle play, if needed. Along the left sideline, the Princeton players were calling encouragement to their team. Slagle hadn't carried the ball yet, Charlie thought. Princeton was famous for their pitchouts to their backs and making end sweeps. He would be ready.

The two teams faced each other. Charlie was positioned on the end. A player ran forward.

The ball was snapped and then pitched back to Slagle. Charlie saw Princeton letting the Amherst players into their line. It was going to be a sweep to his side.

Defensive players often stood in place, fending off the blockers the best they could while trying to stand their ground to stop the man with the ball.

Charlie ran right at the blocker, driving into the startled player.

Jake Slagle, Princeton's star, tried to make a run around Charlie, a foot from the sideline, but Charlie hit Slagle, thigh-high, and with his legs driving, lifted him off the ground, carried him the few feet to the sidelines, and dumped him in the lap of Princeton's coach.

The surprised coach recovered, grinned, then reluctantly shook Charlie's hand.

"Nice hit." Jake rubbed his shoulder, slapped Charlie on the back, then put his arm around Charlie's shoulder as the two superstars strode back onto the playing field.

As he went back into the defensive huddle, Charlie heard the crowd roaring their approval. No matter what they thought of him, no matter what kinds of myths of white superiority they held, they recognized what he had done to Slagle, and he had done it cleanly. He had the first thing he wanted for the day. He had preserved his dignity and proved his point: race has nothing to do with excellence.

The Outstanding Athlete

Charles Drew won more athletic awards than any-one in the history of Amherst College. When he graduated, he received an award as the man who had contributed the most to Amherst in athletics.

Charlie narrowly missed placement on the United States Olympic team in track but received All-American mention as a football halfback in 1924–25. Coach Tuss McLaughry wrote in a December 1952 *Saturday Evening Post* article, titled "The Best Player I Ever Coached," that Charlie "was so valuable in football that he could have played on any team in the country, both in his era and any time since."

"One hint of Drew's phenomenal speed, for the benefit of those who never saw him in action," wrote McLaughry, "is the fact that when this six-foot-one, 195-pounder turned to track, he won the junior national A.A.U. hurdles championship."

"In football he was lightning-fast on the get-away and dynamite on inside plays, plowing on with a 'second effort' that brought him yardage long after he should have been stopped. He threw the old pumpkin-shaped ball farther and with more accuracy than anyone else I ever saw, and was also an excellent receiver. He was equally effective on defense, a true tackler and pass stopper."

"To Amherst men, he will go on in memory as he did on the field."

"Okay, men," he called to his team. "Now that they know we can play, let's go on and win this game."

***

Charlie wasn't always able to win over bigots.

On one occasion, after a game in which Charlie had contributed on both offense and defense to Amherst's win, the team traveled by bus to Boston, where they were scheduled to spend the night. The team was still bringing their gear into the lobby when the hotel manager called Coach McLaughry over to the desk. "There's a problem."

"We have reservations," McLaughry said. "It's under the school's name, Amherst."

"Yes, I have the reservations." The manager pointed at Charlie, Monty, Cook, and Hastie. "They can't stay here. They're colored."

The lobby was silent. "In that case, no one else is staying either," Coach McLaughry said firmly. "We'll take our business elsewhere."

"But what am I going to do with all these rooms I saved for you?" the manager argued angrily.

The coach and the team ignored him as they silently walked back to their bus.

4

KITCHEN-TABLE SURGERY

A month later, in October 1925, Drew looked out a hospital window. The trees on the road below were ablaze with yellow leaves. He decided that New England in the autumn outdid anything he had ever seen in Washington, D.C.

October was also the best time of year to run track, play football, baseball, and basketball, compete in swim meets, and here he was stuck in a hospital bed for a week!

For a brief moment Charlie felt sorry for himself, sorry he wasn't outside enjoying the Fall and playing his favorite sports.

He sat up in the hospital bed and grinned as his friends entered the room.

"I'll bet you feel pretty dumb letting that guy bury his cleat in your thigh," Monty kidded him.

"Sort of makes you want to give up football, doesn't it?" Hastie laughed.

"You just wait until I get out of here. I'll show you some football."

"You know that photograph in your room?" Monty said. "The one that pretty girl back home sent you?"

"What happened?" Charlie was suspicious.

"You know John Coolidge?"

"How could I forget him. His dad is the President of the United States."

"We caught him sneaking in your room trying to steal it."

They all laughed.

"Thanks for looking out for me." Charlie was so happy to be with his friends.

"The year is 1924." Cook pretended to be an announcer, using his fist as a microphone. "It's the Amherst-Wesleyan game. There are just a few minutes left. The score stands at 10-6."

Monty dashed to the window, Hastie to the door.

"Amherst is losing!" Cook announced. "Suddenly, Charlie gets the ball and throws it." Monty held his arms up as if he were the goal post.

"The ball is high," Cook announced. "Five yards. Ten yards. Twenty yards." Hastie pretended to be the ball and ran up to the window. "Thirty-five yards. Touchdown. Game! Amherst wins."

Charlie picked up the ukulele Cook had brought with him and strummed a tune. "Do you recognize this?" he asked.

"'Charlie's Blues,'" Cook said laughing. "I think that's the only song you know how to play."

"Why mess with a good thing, not that my writing it has anything to do with it. Okay, Cook. How about this one, the one you, Monty, and I wrote, 'Sweetheart of All My Dreams'?" Charlie queried.

The boys sang a stanza. Then Charlie pleaded, "Hastie, just hum, don't sing. You're a monotone. We worked really hard writing this song."

They all laughed.

"Wasn't it your own sister who said, 'Charlie Drew plays the sax and the piano loudly and badly'?" Hastie said.

Charlie strummed the opening bars of "Omega, Dear," the song he and Cook wrote. Their fraternity, Omega Psi Phi, eventually adopted it as their national anthem.

Charlie was so busy entertaining his friends that he didn't notice the doctor standing in the doorway.

"All right, young men. Visiting hours are over."

"Hey, Charlie, we're thinking about you." Hastie threw an imaginary football to his bedridden friend.

"I'll be back tomorrow," Monty said. "Are you sure there's nothing you want me to bring you?"

"He needs the picture of that pretty girl from D.C. before Coolidge steals it again." Cook laughed.

"All right. All right." A nurse came in and ushered the boys out of the room. "You heard the doctor. Visiting hours are over."

The doctor took Charlie's pulse. "You've got some good friends there."

"They're good guys," Charlie agreed, smiling.

"I understand you're the young man who isn't sure if he

Richard Thomas Drew with his two sons, Charles (right) and Joe. (Charles Drew Papers/Moorland-Spingarn Research Center, Howard University.)

wants to be an athlete or a doctor?" The kindly man looked at Charlie.

"Yes, sir."

"What interested you in medicine?"

"My little sister Elsie died in 1920." With the back of his hand he brushed away the tears in his eyes. "Little children should not have to die, sir."

The doctor began to take his blood pressure. "How are your grades?"

"I'm not like my friends Cook and Hastie. Cook made the honor society, Phi Beta Kappa." He grinned. "Cook said that if Hastie flunked anything, he'd probably just lay down and die from shame. But my grades are sort of okay."

"What does 'sort of okay' mean?"

"I get good grades in chemistry and biology. I guess I need to put more time into my studies and less into sports."

"You're right. Medical schools don't need football stars. They only accept students who graduate at the top of their class.

"If you think you're able to walk a bit, I'll show you something of what a doctor's life is like."

The doctor helped Charlie stand on his crutches.

Charlie was annoyed at how slowly he walked. He was thankful that the doctor was willing to walk at a slow pace. Left foot, crutch, left foot, crutch. It had taken him a long time before he was able to learn how to hobble along with these things.

As they walked down the hall, two nurses passing by in the other direction smiled at Charlie and greeted the doctor.

They stopped outside a small room and looked in. A man and a woman lay quietly on cots facing one another. The man seemed to be a farmer. Clumps of caked, brown mud were on the toes of his boots. The knees of his heavy pants were faded, probably from many washings. There was a grease stain on the pocket.

A white sheet had been laid across the woman. She looked weak. Her arm lay across her chest.

"That's the farmer's wife," the doctor whispered to Charlie.

Charlie watched as a nurse used a syringe to take blood from the man. Then she walked across the room and injected the blood into the woman. When the syringe was empty, she withdrew it, walked back across the room, and inserted it back into the farmer's arm to get more blood.

"When someone is injured, we have to give them blood right away. Otherwise they can go into shock or even die," the doctor told Charlie.

They walked into another room. The doctor handed Charlie an instrument. It looked like scissors but there was a notch on the tip. Charlie put his fingers through the finger holes, then handed it back to the doctor.

"These are suture scissors, Charlie. It's an instrument we use to cut the thread when we sew people up after surgery. It's made of steel so that it can be sterilized."

"Sterilized means you heat them at a very high temperature to make sure they are really clean and germ-free, right?"

"Yes. We used to use instruments with wooden handles. You can imagine how dangerous those were. Germs from

Most Black Doctors Graduated from Howard University or Meharry Medical College

In Drew's day, most medical colleges in the United States refused to accept black applicants. A few, such as Harvard and Case Western, accepted one or two a year.

At least 85 percent of the black doctors in the United States graduated from either of the two predominately black medical colleges, Meharry Medical School (founded in 1876) in Nashville, Tennessee, or Howard University's College of Medicine, which graduated its first class in 1871 — two black men and three white men. The following year, the graduating class included a woman. For many years it was the only interracial university with professional schools of medicine, dentistry, law, and pharmacy.

Howard University was one of the first universities in the United States to open its doors to people of all races and genders, an unusual idea in the 1870s.

Today, it remains a private university that attracts students and faculty from the Caribbean, Africa, South America, and Asia.

infected blood would get into the wood and from there go into the patient's wounds."

The doctor handed Charlie a pair of thin rubber gloves. "Another new invention?"

"Yes. We want to keep everything as sterile as possible. Even though we teach our doctors and nurses to scrub their hands thoroughly, we don't want anything to infect the patient's wounds."

"So sterilization is really important," Charlie said.

"Vital," the doctor said, nodding.

"What about blood transfusions? Do they always keep people from dying?" Charlie asked.

"No." The doctor shook his head sadly. "Far too many die. Far too many. And we don't know why. One day, a way will be found, but right now, this is the best we can do."

The next day Monty came to visit. Their other friends had exams. Charlie told him what he had seen the day before. "Now I understand how important it is to keep the operating room, surgical instruments, and the patient's wounds germ-free."

"That makes sense," Monty said. "Maybe that's why so many poor people die. Sometimes they don't have the money to go into hospitals for surgery, or they live too far from a hospital. So doctors come to their homes and operate on them on their kitchen tables."

"How clean can that be?" Charlie was shocked.

"And far too many colored people die because many hospitals won't admit colored patients," Monty told him. "Even though Daniel Hale Williams performed the world's first open-heart surgery in Chicago in 1893, most hospitals won't allow him to perform surgery because he's colored. He had to operate on patients in his office. Then he opened Provident Hospital in Chicago. That's where he is now. Provident accepts doctors, nurses, and patients of all races."

"Like Freedmen's Hospital back home in D.C."

"Yes. My parents told me that Dr. Dan, that's what people call him, came to D.C. and modernized Freedmen's

THE LINK BETWEEN POVERTY AND ILLNESS IN MODERN TIMES

The highly infectious Ebola Fever is one of the deadliest diseases known. Over 80 percent of the people who catch it can die within two weeks, after experiencing high fever, stomach and chest pain, and sometimes, massive bleeding from all body openings.

Three major outbreaks of Ebola—in 1976 and 1995—were accidentally caused by health-care workers who were supposed to be curing people.

Many African hospitals and clinics can't afford the disposable needles and masks and gloves needed to prevent the spread of disease. Hundreds of people caught Ebola when needles used to inject one infected person were reused on patients who then went home and spread the disease to their families and villages.

In hospitals and labs using modern sterile equipment, Ebola has rarely spread beyond one additional person.

Hospital. He started a school for nurses there too."

"Monty, why do so many patients die from blood transfusions? Blood is supposed to help people, not make them worse."

Monty didn't have an answer.

***

Charlie Drew graduated from Amherst College in 1926. As he walked down the aisle to receive his diploma, he realized that his experience at Amherst had taught him several things, among them the importance of good friends whose values he shared and mentors who could guide his path and open doors for him.

He was determined to become a doctor. But what school would accept him? Most medical schools in the United States only admitted white students.

Even if Charlie were accepted, where would the money come from? His brother Joe and his sisters Nora and Eva intended to go to college. Their father didn't make much money as a carpet layer. Charlie would have to find a way to come up with the money for medical school himself.

5

PEOPLE ARE DIVIDED BY BLOOD, NOT RACE

Twenty-eight-year-old Charles Drew had gotten into medical school, but now it looked like he might not be able to stay. He sat in a tiny rented room in Montreal, Canada, writing a letter to himself.

Suddenly, the door flew open.

"Hey, Charlie, it's New Year's Eve!" A laughing young man stood in the doorway, his curly red hair pushed under a bright blue cap. "What are you doing here? We're all going to Kaufman's for pigs' knuckles and beer. Put your coat on and come with us!"

Outside, bells rang and factory sirens screeched, although the new year, 1932, would not be for another six hours.

Then another young man, with the longest green scarf Charlie had ever seen, stuck his head over the first man's shoulder and made a funny face. Both were students with Charlie at McGill University's College of Medicine.

They came in and flopped on Charlie's bed, bunching up the spread. Alex unwound his green scarf part way, then held up an empty beer stein. "Here's to Charlie Drew. American. Captain of the McGill University track team."

"I'll drink to that," Pierre said, tossing his hat on the bed. "But let's not forget our esteemed friend's title as secretary of Alpha Omega Alpha, the international honor society for medical students."

Alex stood up and tossed his green scarf over his shoulder so that it draped down the back of his brown tweed coat. "Come out and celebrate, Charlie! Four nurses are waiting outside, and Pierre is buying the beer."

Charlie shook his head. He didn't have the money to spend on pigs' knuckles. But he did have his pride. He wasn't going to let them pay his way.

"If you change your mind, Charlie, you know where to find us," Pierre said. Both young men jumped up from the bed and strode out of the room.

Charlie closed the door behind them. He fluffed up his pillow and pulled the bedspread over it. The room might be tiny, but he was determined to keep it neat.

The little room was the most inexpensive one he could find. He stretched out his arms on either side. He could almost touch the opposite walls.

He looked out the window at the snow-covered streets.

Two little boys threw snowballs at each other, then fell into a snowbank, laughing. Alex ran down the street waving Pierre's cap in his hand. The nurses were nowhere to be seen.

Then he sat at his desk and continued writing the letter to himself. He wanted to stay in medical school. He just didn't know how he could do it. Maybe by pouring his heart out on paper he'd find a solution.

When Charlie graduated from Amherst College, he didn't have the money to go to medical school. Because he was one of the top athletes in the country, he was able to get a job at Morgan State College in Baltimore, Maryland, as a coach of the football and basketball teams. He also taught both biology and chemistry. His salary was $1,500 a year and came with free room and board. In the summer he lived with his family in Washington, D.C., and worked as a lifeguard at a local swimming pool.

He had applied to McGill University's College of Medicine in Montreal, Canada. It was one of the best schools in the world. To his delight, he had been accepted. Unlike the medical schools in the United States, the fact that he was an African-American didn't seem to matter.

He supported himself as he had in college, with a part-time job as a waiter and help from his parents.

Then Charlie's father, a carpet layer, lost his job.

The collapse of the stock market and the closing of banks led to the Great Depression of 1929. Millions of Americans lost their homes and businesses. Everything they had in the bank was wiped out. For minorities the situation was worse.

Unemployed men standing in line at a soup kitchen in Chicago during the Great Depression. (National Archives.)

Many of them worked for farmers or were servants. In many places in the South between 60 and 80 percent of African-Americans suddenly found themselves with no way of making a living.

It looked like Charlie was going to have to quit medical school. Howard University had once offered him a job as a coach. Maybe he could work for a few years, help put his brother and sisters through college, and then maybe return to medical school. Maybe.

He wanted to finish medical school with all his heart.

Was that a knock on the door? There it was again. He

took two large steps across the little room and opened the door. One of his professors from the medical school stood in the doorway. "I wanted to tell you about Landsteiner's Nobel Prize and what his discovery means for the theories of blood transfusions," he said in his characteristically abrupt manner, dumping a pile of magazines on the bed, then sitting in Charlie's chair.

"Happy New Year, Dr. Beattie." Charlie laughed in amazement.

"Oh, yes, Happy New Year. Now about Landsteiner. He was awarded the Nobel Prize two years ago in 1930, and no one has done anything about his discovery."

Charlie was intrigued. "Karl Landsteiner?" he asked.

"Yes. He discovered that people's blood is divided into four different groups."

"How does that work for blood transfusions? Doesn't the donor have to be from the same family as the patient, the patient's parent or child? I read one study that said even husbands and wives can exchange blood. But that didn't make too much sense to me. Marriage doesn't make you a blood relation."

"That's been our mistake!" exclaimed Dr. Beattie. "The donor and the patient don't *have* to be related. They don't have to be of the same sex, the same race, or even the same nationality."

Beattie snatched the letter Charlie had been writing. He turned it over and drew a chart on it. Stabbing the pen at the diagram he had drawn, he said, "You see. Here. The blood types have to match. If a person is type O, you have to give him blood from a donor who is type O. The same with these other blood types."

"So that's why so many people die even though they get transfusions from their husbands or parents."

"Exactly!"

"And Landsteiner just discovered this?"

"No, Charlie, and that's what's so shocking. He was just awarded the Nobel Prize for it. He discovered it nearly thirty years ago!"

"Why didn't people use his discovery before now?" Charlie thought of all the people who had died during all those years because they had gotten the wrong type of blood.

"Because no one read it!" Beattie threw the pen back on the desk and stood up.

BLOOD TYPES

Most people in the United States have either type O blood or type A blood. In 1999, 45 percent of the population were type O, 40 percent were type A, 11 percent were type B, and only 4 percent were type AB.

People with type O blood are called *universal donors*, because in an emergency anyone can safely receive their blood. People with AB blood are known as *universal receivers*, because in an emergency they can safely receive any type of blood.

Portrait of Karl Landsteiner, 1931 Nobel Prize winner. (National Library of Medicine.)

"Professor Beattie, is it possible that there are other studies people have done that no one has read?"

"Of course. Anyway, I came up here to bring you those articles you wanted to read on blood research. You asked for some pretty interesting studies."

Beattie went to the door, then turned around as if he had forgotten something. He reached into his pocket to get his gloves. "Oh, yes. These. Your landlady asked me to bring your mail to you." He handed Charlie some letters and left.

Charlie barely heard Beattie close the door behind him. He sat in the chair and tore open the first letter. It was from his mother.

> We have no money to send you, but you must not give up medical school. We're counting on you to finish. Somehow a way will be found. You must believe that.

He sighed. He didn't really expect any money from home, but he had hoped his mother would think of some way he could stay in school.

He looked at the second letter. It was from Tuss McLaughry, his coach at Amherst. Probably congratulating me on getting into medical school, Charlie thought. He was reluctant to open it. He hated the thought of having to write back and tell him that he didn't have the money to stay in school.

He opened the letter and a check fluttered onto the desk. The coach's letter said:

I contacted your friends from Amherst, Charlie. Some of them are doing quite well. I told them you wouldn't accept a gift, so here's a loan. Pay it back when you can.

Charlie held the letter in his hand, unable to believe what he'd read. He read it again to make sure he hadn't misread it. He read it a third time. It was true.

Maybe he could stay in school now. If he only ate one meal every other day, he might be able to make the money last.

Then Charlie opened the third letter. It was from his old friend Bill Hastie.

Charlie grinned, remembering their good times together. Bill was always a perfect student. He had even made the national honor society, Phi Beta Kappa.

Charlie looked down at the letter:

Here's a bit of money to tide you over the rough spots. I'll send the same amount every month.

Charlie shook his head in disbelief, choking back tears. Hastie's father, a government clerk, had died leaving Hastie's mother without much money. Hastie was teaching school and saving his money, hoping to make enough to go to law school. Hastie had put aside his dreams of going to law school so that Charlie could achieve his own dream!

Then Charlie opened the fourth letter. It was a check from the Rosenwald Fund, an organization in the United States that created schools for nonwhite students. (Until

Charlie's Poverty

This is part of the letter Charles Drew wrote to himself that night:

> **Tonight I wanted to join the merrymaking so bad that my very heart ached. I have a dollar and am afraid to spend it. Tomorrow I must eat and the day after. For days now I have not been sure whether I would eat or not.**
>
> **My classmates could not understand why I couldn't go out with them tonight. When I told them I was broke, they simply thought I had overspent my allowance or my check from Dad hadn't come in. They didn't understand that a few dollars from my father would mean an actual sacrifice for the rest of my family.**

the 1970s many communities refused to let minority students attend public schools.)

Charlie sat back in his chair, stunned and speechless. It was more than he could ever have hoped for. He finally had enough money to finish his studies at McGill.

The bells outside rang louder. It was an hour until midnight. It was a Happy New Year after all!

He was determined to follow his dream of being a doctor. His family and friends believed in him. And he believed in himself. Somehow he would find the way to help the world so that people wouldn't have to suffer and die the way Elsie had.

Right now, money was no longer an obstacle. He sure wasn't going to let racism stop him. He thought back to the lesson he had learned at Dunbar High School, "Excellence of performance can overcome racial bias." He would do his best to make it happen.

***

In 1933 Charles Drew graduated from medical school, second in a class of 137 and ranked first in the country in a nationwide test given to graduating seniors of Canadian medical schools. He was a doctor, one of the best!

Now he had a new dream. He wanted further training so that he could become a surgeon, something few minority doctors in the United States had ever achieved.

But he had to find a hospital willing to take a chance on a young black man. He knew that few in the United States would, but he was determined to try.

6

LESSONS FROM A CORPSE

A wing of Montreal General Hospital was on fire!

A terrified young mother stood in an open window on the fifth floor clutching her newborn baby to her chest and screaming in panic as flames shot out of a window on the floor below her.

On the sidewalk below, people huddled together in the knee-high snow. They barely noticed the frigid wind as they listened to the shrieks of the trapped patients.

An old woman on the street began to cry. "Those poor people," she said. "Those poor people."

A young man put his arms around her. "The firemen will save them."

It seemed as if the fire truck had barely pulled up when the men jumped off and ran inside, their fire hoses trailing them.

In another wing of Montreal General Hospital, thirty-year-old Charles Drew was sound asleep, slumped over in a chair, his head resting on the desk in front of him. A patient's chart was under his hand. A pile of similar files was stacked neatly on the corner of the desk.

After graduation from McGill, Drew worked as a resident, or student doctor, at Montreal General Hospital. Hardworking and eager to learn as much as he could, Drew often worked long hours observing and assisting doctors on their rounds and filling out related paperwork, sometimes into the wee hours of the morning.

"Dr Drew! Dr. Drew! Wake up!"

Charlie lifted his head from the desk, but only slightly. His eyes remained closed. "Dr. Drew!" The nurse shook his shoulder again. "Wake up! One of the wings of the hospital is on fire. Everyone is needed!"

Charlie, instantly alert, dashed into the operating room.

The mood in the room was tense. As soon as Charlie came in, he thoroughly washed his hands and put on sterile rubber gloves.

A little girl covered with burns was wheeled in.

A nurse rushed into the room. "Dr. Drew, we took the patient's blood and typed it. It's type O. But there's none available for her."

"Doesn't she have any family here?"

"Only her mother. But she's not type O."

The little girl's breathing grew heavier as she became more listless.

"There's no one with type O blood here," the nurse repeated sadly. "We even asked strangers in the waiting room and everyone on the medical staff. All of those with her blood type gave yesterday to another victim."

Charlie looked at the child. She opened her eyes. They were as blue as the sky on a summer's day. Then she closed them and gave a little sigh. Her pale little hand fell limp by her side.

She was dead.

***

Charlie finally had a chance to sleep the next day. The fire had been extinguished, and the patients had all been taken care of.

When he woke, Charlie went to Dr. Beattie's office. He removed a pile of professional journals and studies from a straight-backed wooden chair and sat down. "Professor Beattie, I want to find out everything there is to know about blood."

"I thought you already had."

"There's more. There has to be." He told Beattie about the little girl who died the night before. "People shouldn't die because there aren't any donors of their type. The way it is now, when people know they are going to have an operation, they come to the hospital with a friend or relative who is their blood type. That person gives the blood that is used during the operation. But when there's an emergency like last night, there may not be a blood donor available."

Drew paused, thinking aloud. "Suppose someone knows they are going to have an operation. Why can't they come into the hospital the week before and have blood taken from them? Then it can be stored and used during an operation."

"Because the blood won't be fresh. It will clot into lumps and be of no use."

What Is Blood Made Of?

Blood carries oxygen and nutrients to all cells in the human body and removes wastes. Blood consists of four parts: red cells, white cells, platelets, and plasma—the liquid that carries the other three parts.

Red blood cells receive oxygen from the lungs and carry it to the rest of the body. The kind of red blood cell you have determines your blood type: O, A, B, or AB.

White blood cells fight off infections by destroying bacteria and producing antibodies.

Platelets play an important role in clotting by plugging holes in blood vessels and releasing chemicals which cause plasma to trap blood cells in clumps. The clumps form blood clots, which stop bleeding.

In addition to its role in carrying nutrients, chemicals, and the other parts of blood, plasma is needed to maintain a person's blood pressure.

"That's what we've been taught." Charlie leaned forward in the chair. "There must be some studies that people haven't read. There must be some doctors somewhere who have found a way to preserve blood."

Beattie paced the room as he thought. He pointed to the pile of magazines Charlie had removed from the chair and neatly stacked in a corner. "Look through those." He told

Charlie the name of the magazine to look for. It was a professional journal written by doctors for doctors.

Charlie found the magazine and handed it to Beattie.

"Before I came to Canada, back when I was living in England, I heard about a study done by two Russians...oh, here it is." Beattie flipped open to a page and handed it to Charlie. "They used the blood of cadavers."

"Corpses?" Charlie wasn't sure he had heard correctly. "They used the blood of dead people?"

"Yes. They drained their blood and mixed it with some chemicals that kept the blood from clotting, but the red cells kept breaking down."

"That's dangerous," Charlie said.

"Of course it is."

"Has anyone else tried this?"

"Not with any success."

"I need to look at all of the studies," Charlie said, paging through the piles of articles and journals.

Beattie noticed the dark circles under the young doctor's eyes. "From the looks of it, what you need is sleep. You young interns and residents work steadily for 36 hours or more and then only get an hour or two of sleep before you're called on to operate again."

"I need to find a way to keep people from dying," Charlie continued, as he studied the table of contents of a journal.

Beattie waved his hand over the stacks of magazines. "Take whatever you want. If you have time to read about ways to preserve blood instead of getting a few hours of sleep, take them."

Beattie closed his eyes and reminisced. "Blood research has come a long way since I was a medical student in England. One of the most important discoveries, to my mind, is that we now recognize the importance of sterilizing instruments."

Charlie thought back to his days at Amherst and the doctor who had taught him the same lesson.

"It wasn't too long ago that the only method we knew of giving a patient blood was to place donor and recipient side by side. A tube was inserted in the donor so that their blood flowed into the patient lying on an adjoining cot."

Beattie scrutinized the eager young doctor. "You'll be a surgeon soon. What are your plans?"

"I'm going back to Washington. Hopefully I can get a job at Howard University. My goal is to open doors for minority doctors who want to be surgeons."

Beattie frowned. "You have a brilliant mind, Charlie. You should go into blood research."

Charlie didn't answer. He and Dr. Beattie had had this discussion several times. There was no way he could make this Englishman understand the obstacles minority doctors and medical students faced in the United States.

7

"NOW WE HAVE TO BATTLE BLOOD"

Dr. Charles Drew, professor at Howard University's College of Medicine, gathered up the papers from his desk. Class was over and he was due in surgery soon. But he was surrounded by eager students. Some had questions they wanted to ask. Others just wanted to hear anything he had to say. He looked at his watch. "This is the last question," he said.

Drew was one of the top surgeons at Freedmen's Hospital. Throughout Drew's life, it was the only public hospital in Washington, D.C., where nonwhite doctors could practice. (Today, it is known as Howard University Hospital.)

"...so fluid balance is important in our work with blood transfusions," Drew was finishing his answer when he

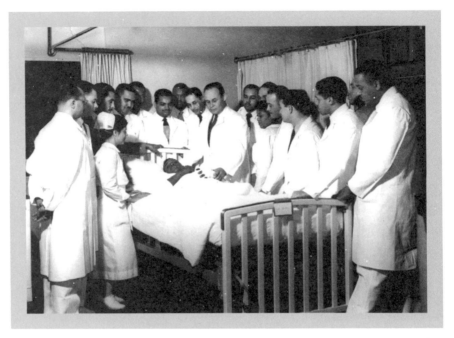

Dr. Drew teaching students at Freedmen's Hospital, Washington D.C. (Charles Drew Papers / Moorland-Spingarn Research Center, Howard University.)

noticed a disturbance at the door. Dr. Numa Adams, the Dean of the College of Medicine, was elbowing his way past the students.

"Gather round, future doctors," Dean Adams said as he strode to the front of the room and turned to face them all. "As you know, Meharry Medical School down in Nashville, Tennessee, and our own Howard University's College of Medicine are the only schools in this country that accept all qualified students, regardless of their race, nationality, or gender. But even now, in this enlightened age of 1938, there are few hospitals other than our own Freedmen's Hospital that offer internships to young colored doctors."

Several students nodded in agreement.

"After you complete an internship, where can you turn to complete your residencies, which are critical if you want to pursue a medical specialty like surgery?"

No one had an answer.

"Well, I'm happy to say that we've set up a residency program right here at Howard University's College of Medicine in partnership with Freedmen's Hospital!"

The students whispered excitedly among themselves.

Drew broke in. "I'd heard rumors that this might happen. This really is excellent news. How is the program being funded?"

"By the Rockefeller Foundation. The funding will be used to train our teachers so they can run the residency program," Dean Adams said meaningfully, looking Drew squarely in the eye. "In fact, Professor Drew, that is why I have come today."

Drew looked astonished but pleased.

"I'm delighted to say that you've been granted a two-year leave of absence to study surgery at New York's Columbia University, so that you can come back and lead our young people."

***

Harlem was an exciting place to be, Drew thought as he strolled up Manhattan's 125th Street in late March 1939. Too bad he didn't have a steady girl to show him around town.

He'd had an early dinner with an older man, Dr. Mass, a graduate of Meharry Medical School. The doctor's wife had invited her two young nieces. Drew was polite, but neither young woman held his interest.

The two men and Dr. Mass's grandson, Walt, were taking an after-dinner stroll past the Apollo Theater.

"That sounds like jazz," Drew said, stopping on the sidewalk to listen.

"It's probably Count Basie's band," the older man said. "They must be rehearsing for tonight's performance."

"It's Duke Ellington," Walt whispered to Drew. "Grandpa doesn't know everything. He just thinks he does." Both were used to the old man's ways and indulged him.

A block from the Hotel Theresa, a man stood on a wooden box. The crowd of people listening to him cheered. "There may be another war," the speaker said. "And if there is, they must let us fight for our country. They must let us enter the Air Force and become pilots. They must let us enter the Navy and become sailors."

"They say we're not smart enough to be sailors," a man in the crowd yelled. "They say we need white commanders to lead us." There were angry shouts of agreement among the crowd.

"And they have all these war industries jobs open now," another man shouted. "But they won't hire colored people. It's whites only. If America's leaders are so mad at the way Hitler's trampled minorities abroad, let them practice what they preach by ending racism here at home!"

Another man in the crowd agreed. "The United States needs to end segregation."

"We must stand together and fight Hitler," the speaker boomed.

"Jesse Owens showed Hitler!" someone shouted.

"The Olympics were held in Nazi Germany in 1936," Dr. Mass reminded his grandson. "Hitler wanted to prove that his people were what he called a 'master race.' Jesse Owens, a Negro, won four gold medals. Hitler was so mad he left the stadium and never presented them to Mr. Owens."

The speaker shouted, "Now that Hitler's invaded Czechoslovakia we need to..."

"Why should we go to Europe and fight?" someone shouted. "We need to stay in the U.S. and fight segregation."

People began to stop listening. They started walking away. Most Americans were angry that Hitler was invading small European countries, but no one wanted the United States to get involved. No one wanted a repeat of World War I, the Great War.

The three men walked down Lenox Avenue.

"Blood transfusions haven't changed much since the Great War," the old man said. "Back then, too many men died because we couldn't get fresh blood to them. Hitler may win this war if we can't find a way to preserve and transport blood to injured soldiers. Drew, doctors have battled disease and won. Now we have to battle blood."

"I'm not sure I understand you," Drew said.

"In the past, more soldiers died of disease than from gunshot," Mass answered. "For instance, during the

Hitler and the Master Race

Adolf Hitler, Germany's leader and the head of its Nazi party, believed in the racial superiority of whites, in particular "pure" Germans, views that were similar to those of many white Americans. Some people in both nations believed whites were biologically superior to all other people. However, Hitler proclaimed that all "inferior" people should be exterminated, a philosophy the United States was against. Hitler ordered the death of millions of Jews, gypsies, nonwhites, the mentally ill, and anyone who disagreed with his philosophy.

In 1939 Hitler's troops began to storm through Europe, taking one country after another. The United States was dismayed, but it was determined not to enter the war.

However, American factories did step up their production of war products, and these were sold or lent to America's allies. Most factories still refused to hire nonwhites.

American Civil War, twice as many men died of typhoid and dysentery as from their wounds. We have disease licked. Now we need to find some way to get blood to wounded soldiers. We need a blood source that can be preserved."

"A blood source that can be preserved," Drew repeated.

"You know, we Negro doctors have a hard time up here,"

Dr. Mass said. "I came to New York from North Carolina, but it's not much better here than in the South."

They were now standing in front of a hospital. The old doctor pointed at it with his cane. "This place is in the center of Harlem and they have no Negro physicians on staff. I applied to them for privileges so that I could treat my patients there. They refused. Most hospitals in New York are like that. When Dr. Louis Wright, an honors graduate of Harvard Medical School, became the first colored doctor at Harlem Hospital in 1919, several white doctors resigned in protest. How many Negro doctors are there now? I'll bet you're the only colored person at Columbia Presbyterian." The old man laughed. "I'll bet even the janitors are white."

Drew didn't know what to say. From what little he had seen since his arrival in New York City, Dr. Mass was right.

Dr. Mass put his hand on Drew's shoulder. "We need young men like you. You learn everything Columbia University has to teach you, then you go back to Howard University and teach those young fellows, like my grandson here. Train them to be the best. They can't keep us out of the hospitals forever."

8

IT'S
WHAT'S INSIDE
THAT COUNTS

Months later Charles Drew was still thinking about Dr. Mass's words, "A blood supply that can be preserved." Drew pondered the problem as he strolled through New York City's Central Park. By his side was his wife.

A year after Drew started work at Columbia Presbyterian Hospital, he had met Lenore Robbins. They were married in September 1939 in her hometown of Philadelphia, Pennsylvania.

Charles Drew held his wife's soft hand as they watched children fly kites in the mild wind. Most of the boys and girls had a hard time keeping the kites up in the air. They fluttered in the breeze, then fell to the earth. But one boy wearing a striped shirt had three kites in the air at the same time.

"He reminds me of you," Lenore squeezed her husband's hand affectionately. "Most people have a hard time doing one job well. You do three. When Howard University gave you a two-year leave of absence to accept this fellowship, you couldn't possibly have known how much time and work was involved."

Drew was an assistant surgeon at Columbia Presbyterian Hospital. For most people, working in the operating room was a full-time job. But Drew and one of his professors, Dr. John Scudder, had also set up a laboratory and were conducting experiments with blood.

Lenore helped. She kept records for them as a laboratory assistant. The research in the laboratory was Drew's second full-time job.

Drew's third full-time task was working on an advanced degree, a doctorate. In order to earn it, he was writing a dissertation, a long research paper. The paper would eventually be 250 pages long and would include everything that was known about the preservation of blood.

Charles and Lenore walked through the zoo, past the lions and tigers. They stopped in front of a caged panther who was pacing back and forth.

"He probably wants his freedom," Drew said. "Lenore, this war in Europe is terrible. Hitler is rounding people up, locking them in buildings that aren't even as sanitary as this cage, and starving them to death."

"All because they're 'different' and inferior in his eyes." Lenore shook her head sadly. "It's so shocking."

"Hitler's no scientist," Drew said angrily. "He doesn't know what he's talking about. There is no such thing as a 'master race' or a superior race of people, as he claims. We all share the same biological traits that make us distinctly human, including an incredible brain that allows us to reason and feel. There's no basis in science for some of the claims Hitler makes."

Charles Drew c. 1940. (National Library of Medicine.)

A vendor with a bright red wagon was selling little brown paper bags of peanuts. Drew bought a bag, and the couple shared it as they walked into the children's zoo.

As soon as they sat down on a bench, a fat brown squirrel scampered across the pavement and sat in front of them on his hind legs. Lenore laughed as she threw a nut to him.

He snatched it and ran away.

"Some people think Hitler might invade France," Lenore said.

"It's possible. Most think it could never happen. But we need to be ready. European soldiers die daily, many of them needlessly, because there's no way we can get fresh blood to them on the battlefield in time. When they finally get to a hospital, hours later, it's too late."

The couple's attention was drawn to a pretty little girl petting a bleating baby lamb in the children's zoo. She wore a blue dress with ruffles on the sleeves and laughed delightfully. "I hope we have little girls," Lenore said. "Maybe a little boy too."

"That little girl makes me think of my sister Elsie. I told you she died during the Doomsday Flu. She also reminds me of a patient in Montreal who died because no donor could be found with her blood type."

The squirrel was back. Lenore looked in the bag for another peanut.

"There must be a way to preserve blood so that a supply can be stored in case of future accidents," Drew said. "We've tried all sorts of experiments."

Lenore threw the last peanut to the squirrel.

"We kept blood in different preservatives. But after a while it became toxic, which means it spoiled and was too dangerous to be of use.

"We looked at white blood cells. They fight infections and bacteria."

"And red blood cells?" Lenore asked.

"Those are the troublemakers. They are the essence of blood, but they cause the transfusion and storage problems. When we refrigerate blood, the red cells spoil in about a week."

Lenore watched the squirrel. The broken shell lay scattered on the ground. The squirrel sat on its hind legs and nibbled on the nut.

"What's the part of blood that has the vital components?" Drew thought out loud as he stared at the broken shell and nut. He thought about the problem as Lenore crumpled up the empty bag and threw it in a trash bin.

Suddenly, the answer came to him. He stood up so fast that the squirrel scampered away. "It's plasma! We've been trying to preserve and store whole blood. That's been our problem. We should focus our attention on plasma!"

"But does plasma have the necessary nutrients?"

"Yes, and an additional advantage of using plasma instead of whole blood is that it can be given to almost any patient. The blood types don't have to match because plasma has no red blood cells!"

"You mean someone with O type blood, for instance, can receive plasma from any blood group?" Lenore wasn't sure she heard right.

Lenore Drew Remembers Her Husband

In the Spring of 1939, Charles Drew drove to an annual black medical conference in Tuskegee, Alabama. Since most hotels and restaurants in the South refused service to blacks in those days, he stayed with his good friend Mercer Cook, then a professor at Atlanta University in Georgia.

Cook and his wife gave a dinner party. One of the guests was Lenore Robbins, a professor of home economics at Spelman College in Atlanta.

Years later, in an article she wrote about her husband, Lenore said of that evening, "He listened to the hopes that I poured out to him.

"'Just keep dreaming high and we'll make the kind of world we want,' he said.

"Three nights later on his way back north, he roused me at one o'clock in the morning. I went down to Spelman's moonlit campus. He proposed to me then and there. Six months later, we married and began our life together in New York City."

"Yes. Imagine what that means during a war! One of the reasons people have been dying on the battlefield is that they have to be cross-matched. Then they have to wait for the results before they are given blood."

"That must be hard to do on a battlefield," Lenore said,

realizing another problem. "It can take a long time to get an injured soldier through enemy fire back to the hospital. Are you suggesting that the soldier can be helped immediately, right on the battlefield?"

"Yes, if plasma is the answer." Drew's smile spread over his face.

"If it is, think of the lives that can be saved!" He grabbed his wife by the hand. "We're going back to the lab. I remember reading some studies about plasma. Some scientists back in the 1920s discovered that it could be stored for long periods of time and it wouldn't go bad. No one bothered to test the theory and see if it worked."

"How expensive is it to store?"

"That's the beauty of it. It's not that expensive at all!"

By this time, they had reached Broadway. They didn't have money for a cab, so they walked briskly toward the subway. "How long can it be stored Charles?"

"I don't know. That's what we have to find out."

"Do you have to add anything to it before it's usable?"

"I don't know. That's what we have to find out."

"Do you really think plasma might be the answer?" Lenore asked. Before her husband could answer, she smiled. She knew what his answer would be. She said, "We don't know. That's what we have to find out."

9

DREW'S PLASMA THEORY IS TESTED

Hitler's armies continued conquering European countries. On May 15, 1940, Holland surrendered to the Nazis. On May 28, Belgium surrendered.

Many Americans feared that Hitler might invade France next.

A group of scientists called the Blood Betterment Transfusion Association had an emergency meeting in June 1940 to see how they could help save France. One way was to get blood to the fighting men. The question was how?

The top doctors in blood research attended the meeting. Dr. John Scudder, a member of the board, brought along his star student, Dr. Charles Drew.

One after another, the authorities presented their ideas, but none of them seemed workable.

Then Charles Drew spoke. He agreed that blood should be collected to send to France, but he suggested a radically new idea. Plasma should be taken from the blood and sent abroad.

It was an idea that had never been tested before.

Drew told of the experiments he and his staff had made.

The group was impressed by Drew and agreed that they would look into his theory. Maybe it would work.

After some discussion they decided to create a program and call it "Plasma for France." Blood would be collected, segregated into plasma, and sent to France. Drew's ideas would be put to the test.

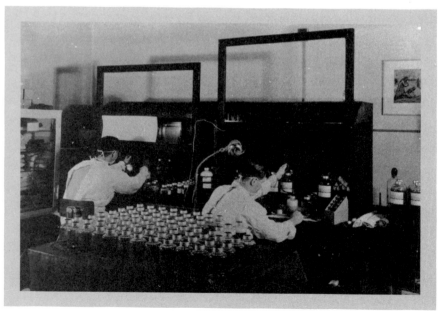

Bottling liquid plasma, Washington, D.C., early 1940s. (National Library of Medicine.)

Drew Was One of the Greatest Scientists of the Twentieth Century

John Scudder, MD, a professor of surgery and Drew's teacher at Columbia University praised Drew in an article called "Practical Genetic Concepts":

> **Drew was naturally great. A keen intelligence coupled with a retentive memory in a disciplined body, governed by a biological clock of untold energy; a personality altogether charming, flavored by mirth and wit, stamped him as my most brilliant pupil. His flair for organization with his attention to detail...a physician who insisted on adequate controls in his experiments...[He was] one of the great clinical scientists of the first half of the twentieth century.**

One thing they all agreed on was that Drew was a scientist worth taking note of.

But Drew's part in the project had ended. He'd completed his fellowship at Columbia University and in June 1940 became the first African-American to be awarded a Doctor of Science in Surgery degree from Columbia University. He wrote to a friend saying that the degree made him feel "like the day after a big race is won, only in medicine it takes much longer."

The Blood Transfusion Betterment Association

In those days people could sell their blood for between $35 and $50, more than most people earned in a week. Because there were so few jobs available, this was the only way many people could earn money during the Depression.

But this method was not safe for the donor or the patients. There were no regulations and no agency making sure the blood was untainted.

In New York City, for instance, the health department learned that professional blood donor bureaus were recruiting some people who were alcoholics, drug addicts, or had communicable diseases.

A group of doctors decided to do something about the situation. They organized the Blood Transfusion

Now it was time to get back to Washington and put his other idea to the test. He believed that doctors, medical researchers, and surgeons could be any color. He intended to help Howard University and Freedmen's Hospital build a program so that young doctors could get the training they needed to become surgeons.

***

On June 14, 1940, the unthinkable happened. The Nazis paraded through the streets of Paris. France had fallen at last.

Betterment Association. Members included Drew's professor at Columbia University, Dr. John Scudder, and Dr. Karl Landsteiner, the Nobel Prize–winning Austrian who was now an American citizen and living in New York City.

The association insisted that donors be tested and that those with communicable diseases or who were addicted to drugs or alcohol not be allowed to donate blood.

They also insisted that donors must have had a recent physical examination. Donors were given a green registration book which they had to present each time they came to sell their blood. The book included the results of the donor's physical examinations and records of when they gave blood.

It happened so quickly that the "Plasma for France" program never got off the ground. Drew's theories didn't have a chance to be tested.

Then Germany started air attacks on Britain. They bombed London and other English cities day and night. Thousands were killed and thousands more were injured. The wounded needed blood, but there wasn't enough.

There was only one thing to do. The Blood Betterment Association sent an urgent telegram.

BANKED BLOOD, THE ANSWER OR JUST A THEORY?

"That procedure went well," Drew congratulated the young doctor. "Keep practicing your suturing exercises."

"You do it so quickly."

"I've had a lot of practice suturing." Drew laughed. "Last night I sewed the arm back on my daughter's rag doll. My wife was impressed by the neat stitches. After all, suturing is sewing up surgical wounds. And, young man, your stitches are still too large. I keep reminding you, use small, tight stitches."

The two men walked down the steps of Freedmen's Hospital. It was late summer, and the midday sun was unbearably hot. Drew made a graceful movement with his fingers, demonstrating that surgeons had to learn how to sew using one hand. The other needed to be free for other things, such as handling the instruments used in an operation. Many future surgeons took a piece of string and practiced tying knots using one hand, over and over.

The young man understood the gesture. "Keep practicing!" he agreed, waving goodbye to Drew as they parted ways.

Drew was still smiling as he walked across the campus to his office. His students were learning quickly. He was pleased with their progress. He was so engrossed in thought that it was a while before he recognized the figure striding across campus toward him.

"Lenore!" he said in surprise.

Dr. Charles Drew with doctors, nurses, and drivers from a mobile unit of the Columbia Presbyterian Hospital. (Charles Drew Papers / Moorland-Spingarn Research Center, Howard University.)

"This just came. I think it's important." She handed him a telegram.

Drew sat down on a stone bench, stunned by what he read. "It's from the Blood Transfusion Betterment Association. They want me to move to New York to supervise a program that they call 'Blood for Britain.'"

He handed his wife the telegram. John Bush, the head of the organization, had written:

> The Board has decided to create a position of Medical Supervisor to act as liaison officer between the Board and the hospitals engaged in processing plasma for shipping to the British Red Cross. I am requested to offer this position and all it involves to you as being the best qualified of anyone.

Lenore returned the telegram to her husband. "England needs blood and so they turned to you, Charles, of course. You're the best man for the job."

"They need thousands of pints of blood," Drew said, beginning to realize the implications of his involvement. "If I accept this job, my discoveries can be put to the test."

"Charles, you've read everything there is to read and spoken to everyone who knows anything about safely preserving blood, from pathologists to chemists and biologists." She paused before continuing, "You are really the only person who can do this. You've been waiting for this chance."

"I'll model it after the Plasma for France program," Drew said, thinking rapidly about what would need to be done. "We'll need to set up blood banks."

"What's a blood bank?"

"A place to store blood, like a bank. It's a term Chicago's Cook County Hospital invented when they set up one three years ago."

"With the Nazis overtaking Europe and now bombing Britain, preserved blood is needed more than ever. If you accept this assignment and your theories about plasma are proven true, millions of lives could be saved."

"That's all they are right now, Lenore, theories," Drew said. "There has never been anything on this immense scale of collecting, testing, preserving, and transporting vast amounts of blood. But I'm convinced it's what needs to be done."

He looked at Lenore and touched her hand. "How can I even think of leaving you and little Roberta? And what about my students?" He read the telegram again and sighed.

"Go to New York," Lenore said, squeezing his hand. "Baby Roberta and I will be fine here. Britain needs you. Millions of deaths can be prevented with your help, Charles."

"If my theories work," Drew said.

11

LIQUID DYNAMITE

Drew arrived in New York on September 1, 1940, and hurried up to Columbia Presbyterian Hospital on West 168th Street where the blood project had been set up.

When Drew took over as the head of the Blood for Britain program, the work had been divided. The New York chapter of the American Red Cross had taken over the responsibility of getting donors, and the Blood Transfusion Betterment Association drew the blood.

One of the first challenges Drew encountered was keeping the plasma free from contamination by bacteria before it arrived in England. Contaminated plasma could kill a recipient, which is why the British often referred to plasma as "liquid death."

Another problem was that there was no uniform method of collecting blood and processing plasma.

Each of the New York City hospitals in the Blood for Britain program was headed by a doctor who had his own

An early experimental blood bank vault. (Charles Drew Papers/
Moorland-Spingarn Research Center, Howard University.)

method of collecting and processing blood and his own idea of
what supplies and equipment should be used. The result was
that at least 14 percent of the plasma was contaminated.

Drew decided to standardize blood collections. First, he made sure the project used well-trained technicians. He believed that if the blood was collected in a careful and sanitary manner, it was less likely to be contaminated.

Then Drew looked at how the blood was drawn and labeled. He developed new rules and guidelines and insisted blood be tested at different stages.

His new procedures worked. None of the newly collected blood was contaminated.

Now the Blood for Britain program needed thousands of people to donate their blood free, rather than expecting payment for it.

Blood for Britain launched a promotional campaign. Advertisements requesting blood donations were placed in buses and on billboards. There was no television yet, but announcements were made on the radio and in newspapers.

The campaign proved to be an outstanding success— 14,566 people volunteered to give blood to help save England.

Then another problem cropped up. Some hospitals had too many donors while others had too few.

The solution was a main office set up at the New York Academy of Medicine on Fifth Avenue. Prospective donors phoned in and were assigned to the hospital closest to them.

Drew's final challenge was how to transport plasma. He soon learned that plasma traveled best and safest in a dried form.

But how to separate plasma from all the blood collected? He read that someone in England had creatively used a cream separator from a dairy to separate plasma from blood. Drew tried one himself and was delighted to find it worked. He ordered several and made some modifications.

Drew and his Blood for Britain program were able to send thousands of lifesaving pints of plasma to England.

The Blood for Britain program successfully ended after it inspired the British to set up their own blood program. The last shipment of plasma from the United States was sent to England on January 17, 1941.

***

Drew wrote an 86-page report on the program. The American Red Cross was so impressed with the success of the Blood for Britain program that they invited Drew to set up blood banks throughout America.

He accepted, recognizing the hurdles the program would have to surmount. Thousands of pints of blood had been obtained for the British. The Red Cross wanted *millions* of pints of blood for America's Armed Forces.

With the organizational skills he'd learned as a coach and professor and the dedication to detail that he had practiced throughout his life, Drew was perfectly suited to the enormous task.

In a few months, Drew helped the Red Cross set up blood banks across America. Eventually, every military base had a blood bank and every hospital had one or had access to one.

Charles Drew's work was done, and he returned to his teaching duties at Howard University in April 1941 and to the young doctors that he was preparing to be among America's finest surgeons.

FAST FORWARD

BLOOD BANKS TODAY

Charles Drew published many articles about blood. His dissertation, "Banked Blood: A Study in Blood Preservation," was described by Dr. John Scudder as "a monumental work, a guide to the founding of blood banks."

Today's blood banks are based on the system Drew originally set up. In 1999 there were more than 5,000 blood banks across the United States; they collect more than 13 million pints of blood every year. They are licensed or registered by the Food and Drug Administration of the United States Department of Health.

A registered nurse working in a blood bank in the United States, 1995. (© Paul A. Souders / Corbis.)

He had been the medical supervisor for Blood for Britain from September 1, 1940, until January 1941. Then from February 3, 1941, until the end of March 1941, he helped the American Red Cross set up blood banks throughout America.

In the less than six months that Dr. Charles Drew had supervised the Blood for Britain program and helped the American Red Cross set up blood banks, blood storage had been revolutionized. Millions of lives had been saved. Hopefully, millions more would be saved in the years to come.

America was still trying to avoid war. But by November 1941, the Nazis had invaded Norway, Denmark, Belgium, Luxembourg, and Holland. Italy, Germany's ally, had occupied Greece, Egypt, and Somalia. Germany and Italy had signed a pact with Japan giving her control of Greater East Asia.

If the United States did enter the war, would Charles Drew's methods work as successfully as they had for Britain? Could enough blood be transported safely to American troops who were shipped overseas?

The answers would come before Christmas.

12

"ALL HELL BROKE LOOSE"

The morning of December 7, 1941, was sunny and clear in the Hawaiian islands, then a territory of the United States. Dr. Joseph Strode, a surgeon in private practice near the U.S. Army base at Pearl Harbor on the island of Oahu, had been up since 5:45 a.m. He'd done an appendectomy at Queens Hospital. Then he strolled over to the auditorium to hear a lecture by a distinguished surgeon from New York City.

Soon after Dr. Strode took his seat, the speaker stepped to the podium and began his talk with a Biblical quote from St. Matthew, "Be ye also ready for in the hour that ye know not..."

Suddenly, the door was thrown open, and a doctor ran in shouting, "Every surgeon is needed at Tripler General Hospital. Now!"

Doctors ran for their cars, still unsure of what had happened. They quickly learned that Japanese planes had

USS Arizona *burning after the Japanese attack on Pearl Harbor.*
(National Archives.)

appeared seemingly out of nowhere. They were bombing the U.S. military airfield and the battleships in the harbor.

***

At seven o'clock that morning a radar operator told his commanders about approaching aircraft on his screen. The officers ignored it, assuming it was the convoy of American aircraft that was due some time that day.

Almost an hour later, at 7:50 a.m., 183 Japanese planes began arriving at Pearl Harbor, dropping bombs and torpedoes on the base. One American survivor recalled, "It was as if all hell broke loose." Obviously, the Japanese hoped a surprise attack would enable them to destroy American aircraft on the ground so the Americans wouldn't be able to get their planes in the air and return fire.

Then, an hour later a second wave of 168 Japanese aircraft appeared, completing the destruction of a total of 347 American military aircraft and several ships. One ship, the *USS Arizona* took 1,177 men with her as she sank. They lie buried inside her today at the *Arizona* Memorial in Pearl Harbor.

All together, 2,300 American military personnel were killed and 1,100 were wounded. (There were also civilian casualities.)

Later that day, when President Roosevelt addressed the nation in a radio address, he said, "It is a date that will live in infamy."

At last, the United States entered World War II.

***

When the military doctors rushed to Tripler Hospital on that fateful morning, they found the entrances, passageways, and corridors full of injured people. There was no place to put the ever-increasing numbers of patients. First, there were 60 wounded, then 80, and soon more. Most were left on stretchers on the floors until even these were full. Soon, many patients were simply left outside on the hospital's lawn, and doctors tended to them there.

There were flesh wounds, torn scalps, and fractured ribs. Many of the wounded were in shock. Some were badly mutilated, and a few had limbs blown off.

Many times that day, as he treated one patient after

FAST FORWARD

DORIE MILLER, AN UNSUNG HERO OF WORLD WAR II

When the Japanese attacked Pearl Harbor, Dorie Miller, Mess Attendant, Third Class, was gathering the laundry on the *USS West Virginia*. At that time, minorities were not allowed to become U.S. Navy sailors, they could only clean up, wait tables, and do laundry.

Two armor-piercing Japanese bombs broke through the ship's deck, and five eighteen-inch aircraft torpedoes were shot into her port side. The ship started to sink.

"Get the captain! The captain's down," someone ordered Miller.

Miller, a former football hero, dashed to the bridge, carried his commander to safety, then manned the fifty-caliber

---

another, Dr. Joseph Strode gave fervent thanks for the existence of the blood bank. Without it, thousands of the wounded would have died.

"When the Japanese attacked Pearl Harbor, adequate plasma was on hand," Lenore Drew wrote. "And of every one hundred wounded men who were given transfusions with it, ninety-six recovered."

Charles Drew's theory about plasma had been put to the test and proven right once again.

Fourteen thousand donations of blood had been obtained for the Blood for Britain program. Fourteen

Browning antiaircraft gun, shooting down several Japanese planes until there weren't any bullets left.

What makes this story even more remarkable is that he had never operated the antiaircraft gun or any other military weapon in his life.

There were write-in campaigns to bring Miller home for a hero's welcome and petitions to send him to the Naval Academy. None were successful. Nor was Miller promoted to anything above messman status. Two years later, on November 24, 1943, the ship Miller was on, the *USS Liscome Bay* was sunk. He was declared missing in action.

Since then, campaigns to remember him have been successful. Although Miller was awarded the Navy Cross by Admiral Chester W. Nimitz on May 27, 1942, many feel he should have been given the Purple Heart. On June 30, 1973, a ship was named after him, the *USS Miller*.

---

million pints were collected by the American Red Cross during World War II.

During the American Civil War of the 1860s, half of all soldiers admitted to hospitals died, but during World War II, only 4 percent did. World War II took more than 50 million lives, but many more would have perished were it not for the blood banks.

Consequently, Drew became one of the heroes of World War II and received many honors. In 1944, he received the Spingarn Medal, the highest award given by the NAACP. In 1981 the United States Post Office issued a first-class stamp in his honor.

Will Negro Blood Turn Me Black?

One of the ironies of Drew's career was the stance of the military and the American Red Cross on the blood of African-Americans.

Drew left the Red Cross in March 1941 and returned to his teaching position at Howard University. That same year, months before the United States entered World War II, the Army ordered the Red Cross to accept only the blood of white people.

Drew, his friend Judge William Hastie, and others learned of this outrage and protested.

The Army relented after the United States entered World War II that December, but it segregated the blood.

Drew and Hastie protested that policy too, but the military refused to budge.

In an article in the December 28, 1941, edition of *The New York Times,* with the headline "Army Navy Ban on Colored Blood Downright UnAmerican and Stupid," a representative of the Red Cross said:

> No soldier who is about to die is going to arise from his bed or the operating table and say, "Stop doctors! Wait a minute. If you are not absolutely positive that not one single drop of Negro blood is in that blood, let me die."

Despite agreeing with Drew and other scientists that segregating blood made no scientific sense, the Red Cross followed the orders of the military. For the remainder of the war and for years after, donated blood

A crew of six African-American servicemen who were given the Navy Cross for standing by their gun while under enemy attack in the Philippines c. 1945. (National Archives.)

was labeled either white or AA for Afro-American. (It is believed that this practice continued in many Southern communities through the 1970s.)

Some people believed that receiving the blood of a criminal would make them criminals. Along the same lines, many believed that receiving the blood of a Negro would turn them into African-Americans.

In an interview with a newspaper, *The Chicago Defender,* Charles Drew said:

> The question arises, Is there a difference between the blood of different races? Is it possible to transmit the traits and characteristics of one race to a member of another race by means of blood transfusions?

> There are many who have a fear born of ignorance that the blood of a Negro carries with it the possibility of their offspring having dark skin and other characteristics of the Negro race...this prejudice...is founded on ignorance.

A white woman wrote Drew:

> If the only way to save my son's life is to give him the blood of a Negro, let him die.

At the time, Southern white women hired black women to nurse their babies. White families allowed their babies to drink the milk of a Negro, but they would not accept a transfusion of the same woman's blood.

13

CHARLES DREW TRIUMPHS... AGAIN!

One evening in December 1948, Charles Drew was pacing the floor of his living room in Washington, D.C. He went over to the window and looked out. His mind was in such turmoil, he didn't notice the sunset.

"Charlie, you promised the children a song," Lenore reminded him.

"And so I did." Drew strode across the room, sat on the piano bench, and played the opening bars to a song he had composed when he was young. He never gave it a title, but all his friends called it "Charlie's Blues."

"What do you want to hear next?" he asked when he finished.

The children, Roberta (age 9), Charlene (age 6), Rhea Sylvia (age 4), and the youngest, Charles Junior (age 2), each called out a different song. He played them all and sang so loudly the children had no idea that he was worried about anything.

Charles Drew with his wife, Lenore, and their four children. (Charles Drew Papers / Moorland-Spingarn Research Center, Howard University.)

"Play something on the saxophone, Daddy," one of the girls said, pulling on his sleeve.

"No, Daddy, play something on the ukulele," her sister chimed in.

"The musicale is over," Lenore said, picking up Charles Junior and taking Sylvia by the hand. "It's bedtime."

The children kissed their father goodnight and dutifully walked up the stairs ahead of their mother.

Lenore was halfway up the staircase when she turned and looked at Drew, who remained deep in thought at the piano bench. "Charlie, it will be all right. I'm sure it will be all right." When he didn't answer, she reminded him, "Will you come up to read the children a story?"

"Of course!" Drew smiled and ran up the stairs to join them.

An hour later, after the children were sound asleep, Lenore sat in the living room sewing buttons on a white shirt.

Drew pulled the drapes closed against the winter night. He sat beside Lenore and tried to read, but he couldn't concentrate. He got up and started pacing again.

"Your students will do all right," Lenore assured him as she pulled white thread through a needle.

"All right won't be good enough." Drew looked at her. "This is it. The American Board of Surgery's examination is what I've been preparing them for all along. But they're competing with graduates of the nation's top medical schools, Lenore, doctors who've had every advantage."

He sat down on the sofa and grabbed her hand. "I don't want them to just do all right. I want them to do their best, to excel. They have to. It will show the world that minorities are as capable of being surgeons as anyone, anywhere. This is what Monty Cobb and I have been working at for all these years."

He stood up and started pacing again.

"There's a coal bin in the basement you've been meaning to attack for some time," Lenore said after a moment's thought.

Drew nodded and walked away. Minutes later, Lenore heard the steady beat of the sledgehammer as he demolished the old wooden crate.

***

The hammering in the basement grew louder. Thank goodness the noise wasn't waking the children, Lenore thought.

Dr. Charles Drew showed a great deal of commitment to his students. (Charles Drew Papers / Moorland-Spingarn Research Center, Howard University.)

Drew Trained Half of America's Black Surgeons

Charles Drew taught at Howard University's College of Medicine from 1936 to 1938 and from 1941 to 1950. The doctors he trained were among the first wave of minorities to become surgeons and specialists, paving the way for many more to follow.

"During the years Drew taught at Howard, more than half of the nation's black surgeons that received certification from the American Board of Surgeons studied directly under him," Lenore Drew wrote. "Today, more than a score of his students are tops in their various specialized fields. Better yet, doors once closed are now open."

The banging went on for fifteen minutes, and then half an hour. An hour passed, and Drew was still hammering away. When the phone rang, he didn't hear it.

Lenore answered, listened attentively, politely thanked the caller, and hung up. Then she sat down in the nearest chair. Tears filled her eyes. She could hardly believe it. It was so surprising!

She composed herself and walked down the stairs to the basement. Drew looked up as she descended.

"Charlie, we just had a phone call. It was Dr. Mordecai

Famous Black Scientists

In 1950 Charles Drew wrote an article about some of the black scientists of his day. He included:

Professor George Washington Carver (1864–1942) of Tuskegee University, best known as the biologist who introduced the world to over three hundred products made from sweet potatoes and peanuts, including peanut butter.

Ernest Everett Just, Ph.D. (1883–1941), a zoologist who did original research in cell division and fertilization.

William Hinton, MD (1883–1959), a professor at Harvard Medical School who developed a test for syphilis which Drew called "one of the most sensitive devised."

Daniel Hale Williams, MD (1856–1931), who performed the first open-heart surgery on July 9, 1893, in Chicago, Illinois. Drew called him the "Father of Negro Surgery."

Percy L. Julian, Ph.D. (1899–1975), who developed synthetic cortisone to help people with arthritis.

Drew ended the article with these words, "There is a teamship which extends beyond science; this team must include all of us who are interested in understanding and in human happiness."

In addition to being a respected teacher and physician, Dr. Charles Drew did important laboratory work on blood and its components. (Charles Drew Papers / Moorland-Spingarn Research Center, Howard University.)

Johnson, the President of Howard University. He learned that your students passed the test and..."

"There's more?"

"Yes. One of your students made #2 on the exam."

Charlie threw down his hammer and let out a whoop.

Lenore sat down. "And Charlie..."

Drew looked at her with concern. "Surely no bad news?"

"Charlie, one of your students made #1. Number one of all the people who took the exam. Charlie, your students took the top two spots!"

Charlie dropped into a chair, speechless. His eyes filled with tears. "First and second," he whispered. "Well, what do you know about that?"

At last, Drew had achieved his lifetime goal! He'd shown that black doctors were smart and capable enough to be surgeons!

14

"ALL THE BLOOD IN THE WORLD"

Charles Drew and his three doctor friends were in a good mood as they piled into the car on the night of March 31, 1950. It would be a long ride from Washington, D.C., to the annual medical conference in Tuskegee, Alabama, but this way they could avoid the humiliation of "Jim Crow" trains.

The men took turns driving.

"I'll take over when we get to North Carolina," Drew offered. "Right now I need a nap. I'm worn out. I was in surgery last night and all of today. Then I spoke at the student council banquet. I don't remember the last time I saw a bed!"

They stopped in Richmond, Virginia, for coffee. When they got back in the car, it was Drew's turn to drive. The others rested their eyes. They'd had a long week, too.

The sun was shining brightly at eight o'clock that morning, April 1, 1950. The car whizzed past fields near Burlington, North Carolina. Drs. John Ford and Walter Johnson were sleeping soundly in the back seat. Dr. Samuel Bullock was dozing in the passenger seat next to Drew when he felt a bump. Instantly awake, he realized that "the sky wasn't where it should have been." Drew had fallen asleep at the wheel!

Bullock shouted, "Hey, Charlie!"

But it was too late.

The car swerved off the road and flipped over and over, three times.

Dr. Johnson had a slight injury. He helped Dr. Bullock out of the car. Bullock was wedged under the car's dashboard. He only had a cut on his hand.

Drs. Johnson and Bullock went to look for Dr. Ford.

They found him sitting on the grass ten feet away from the car, holding his arm. The doctors realized he'd broken it. They gently put his left hand between the buttons of his shirt, like a sling.

But where was Drew?

Drs. Johnson and Bullock found him on the ground near the left front wheel of the car. His right foot was caught under the brake pedal. His leg was almost severed, his chest was crushed. He was in shock and barely breathing.

Passing motorists and a highway patrol officer stopped to help. A black farmer, Ed Farmville, phoned for an ambulance, then called Washington Irving Morris, the principal of the black elementary school. "You need to come down here," Mr. Farmville told him. "Some Negro doctors have been killed. There's a terrible wreck."

The ambulance came, removed Drew from under the car, and rushed him to Alamance General Hospital near Burlington.

***

Although there were three black doctors in the Burlington area, none had ever been allowed to practice at Alamance General Hospital.

The hospital had 48 beds. Two of them were assigned to black patients. Both were in the basement, as was the hospital's emergency room.

Dr. Ford's broken arm was cared for, and he was sent to one of the black beds in the basement, where he stayed for two days.

But what about Drew? What would they do about him?

A white surgeon, Dr. George Carrington, owned the hospital. Like Drew he was tall, had brown hair, and sometimes turned red in the face. He stared at the injured man as Dr. Johnson helped the ambulance assistant wheel Drew into the emergency room. "Is that Dr. Charles Drew?" Carrington asked in astonishment.

"Yes," Dr. Johnson said. "We had an accident on the highway."

Instantly realizing the gravity of the situation, Dr. Carrington boomed out orders.

Dr. Charles Kernodle, a general surgeon, and his brother, Dr. Harold Kernodle, an orthopedic surgeon, rushed to the emergency room to help Carrington. Dr. Harold

Kernodle, a military surgeon during World War II, later said that he knew that Drew was "the founder of plasma. We knew what we were dealing with."

Charles Kernodle knew of Drew's contribution to medicine from a friend, a hematologist who worked with Duke University's blood bank in the 1940s.

The three white doctors worked heroically on Drew for two hours, but his chest was so damaged by the crash that blood couldn't get to his heart. They discussed transferring him to the more modern hospital at nearby Duke University, but before action could be taken, Drew died.

A nurse who worked on Drew later said, "There was nothing anyone could do. He was torn up too bad."

As one of the doctors in the car later said, "All the blood in the world could not have saved him."

Charles Drew was dead at the age of 45.

CONTINUING WHAT CHARLES DREW STARTED: "DREAMING HIGH"

At Dr. Charles Drew's funeral, Dr. Mordecai Johnson, the President of Howard University, said that Drew's life was one "which crowds into a handful of years significance so great men will never be able to forget it."

Drew was an extraordinary person, but his life demonstrates that we can all achieve our dreams if we keep "dreaming high."

Charles Drew faced the roadblock of discrimination but didn't let it stop him. He succeeded because he worked hard, believed in his goal, and because he had the support of a loving family and good friends, teachers, and colleagues.

One of Drew's students, Dr. LaSalle Lefall, former head of the Department of Surgery at Howard University's College of Medicine, was greatly influenced by Drew. "If young people follow Dr. Drew's example and strive for excellence, that excellence will be recognized despite artificial barriers as gender, religion, and race," he said.

***

Mrs. Lenore Drew poses with the Director of the National Institutes of Health at the unveiling of a bust and exhibit honoring Dr. Charles R. Drew, "Father of the American Blood Bank," June 1, 1981. (National Library of Medicine.)

Dr. Charles Drew opened the door so that more minorities could become surgeons and specialists.

Will you be one of the people who will continue to open doors for others, who will dream high and excel?

Opportunities in medicine and science are expanding. Discoveries are being made daily.

Many medical mysteries have yet to be solved. New ones keep arising—AIDS and the Ebola virus, for example, and we still don't have a cure for the common cold, nor can we yet prevent or cure all cancers.

New specialties in health care are constantly evolving. Many do not require a medical degree.

Lawyers defend the rights and needs of patients, doctors, and medical researchers.

Politicians and activists get laws passed that help patients and the general public.

Business managers and administrators run hospitals, doctors' offices, and health care plans.

People are needed to teach science to children who will grow up to be physicians. Librarians are needed to help children find books about health and help doctors find research articles.

Writers and medical illustrators are needed to explain new health discoveries.

People without college degrees can take special courses to become professionally certified as respiratory therapists, paramedics, and nurses' aides.

Students can work as volunteers in blood banks, hospitals, and nursing homes.

Today, most colleges and medical schools admit people of all ethnicities. Yet despite Drew's accomplishments, there are still people who continue to believe racist ideas. Hopefully, the day will soon come when bigotry will end.

We cannot waste genius. We need people of all races, nationalities, and economic backgrounds to help make the world a healthier place.

As Charles Drew said, "We need to keep dreaming high so we can make the kind of world we want."

TIMELINES

The World During Charles Drew's Life

1904   Theodore Roosevelt becomes President of the United States. Work begins on the Panama Canal.

1909   The National Association for the Advancement of Colored People (NAACP) is created.

1910   The Union of South Africa is established as a white nation in a country where the majority of the citizens are nonwhite.

1912   The "unsinkable ship," the *EMS Titanic*, hits an iceberg and sinks in the Atlantic Ocean. Seven hundred twelve passengers and crew are rescued, but 1,513 people die.

1913   Henry Ford mass-produces cars in Detroit, Michigan, on the first assembly line.

1914   The Panama Canal opens. World War I begins on June 28, when Germany declares war on Russia and France. Britain then declares war on Germany, and Austria declares war on Russia.

1915   The Ku Klux Klan, a secret terrorist organization founded in 1866 that uses violence to support its theory of "white Protestant supremacy," boasts a national membership of 4 million this year.

1917   The United States enters World War I by declaring war on Germany on April 6, and on Austria-Hungary, December 7.

1918   The "Doomsday Flu" kills 22 million people around the world. After almost four years of fighting, World War I ends November 11. The United States and its allies win.

1919	The League of Nations is created to prevent any more world wars. The first Pan-African conference is held, led by the American W.E.B. DuBois.
1920	The Nineteenth Amendment to the U.S. Constitution gives women the right to vote. Gandhi begins a nonviolent movement in India to win independence from Great Britain.
1927	Charles Lindbergh's solo flight from New York to Paris, May 20–21, is the first nonstop flight across the Atlantic Ocean.
1929	The stock market crashes on October 28, leading to the Great Depression. Millions of people lose all their money and millions more their jobs.
1935	The Social Security Act is passed by Congress, giving Americans a guaranteed income in their old age.
1939	On September 1, Germany invades Poland, starting World War II. On September 3, England and France declare war on Germany.
1940	Germany conquers France. Japan becomes an ally of Germany and Italy when it signs a treaty with them called the Tripartite Pact.
1941	The Japanese attack the U.S. base at Pearl Harbor in Hawaii on December 7, and the United States enters World War II.
1945	Germany surrenders to the Allied Forces (England, France, the United States, among others) in April. The United States drops its new weapon, the atom bomb, on Japan on August 3 and again on August 6. Japan surrenders. World War II is over.
1947	Jackie Robinson joins the Brooklyn Dodgers, becoming the first black player on a white, American major league baseball team.
1948	By a mandate of the United Nations, the state of Israel

is created in the state of Palestine. The transistor is invented. The University of Arkansas admits its first black medical student, Edith Irby Jones.

Charles Drew's Life

1904 Charles Drew is born in Washington, D.C., on June 3.

1912 The terms *universal donor* and *universal recipient* are coined when it is discovered that it is safe to give group O blood to patients of any blood group and that blood from all groups can be given to group AB patients.

1920 The National Medical Association convinces all-white Harlem Hospital to begin hiring black doctors.

1921 It is discovered that insulin can help treat diabetes.

1922 Drew graduates from Dunbar High School and enters Amherst College in Amherst, Massachusetts.

1924 The National Medical Association convinces all-white Tuskegee Hospital to appoint four black doctors.

1926 Drew graduates from Amherst College.

1928 Penicillin is discovered.

1930 Austrian physician Karl Landsteiner is awarded the Nobel Prize for his discovery of three human blood groups: A, B, and O. (AB is discovered later.)

1931 Drew becomes captain of the track team at McGill University in Montreal, Canada, where he is studying to be a doctor.

1932 The first blood bank is established in a Leningrad hospital.

1933 Drew receives his MD, graduating second in a class of 137 at McGill University.

1936–1937 Drew is an instructor in pathology at Howard University's College of Medicine and an Assistant in Surgery at Freedmen's Hospital.

1937	The term *blood bank* is first introduced and applied to a laboratory that stores blood in Chicago's Cook County Hospital.
1938	Drew is awarded a fellowship to Columbia University in New York City.
1939	Drew marries Lenore Robbins on September 23. Using blood that Charles Drew sent him, Karl Landsteiner and others discover the Rh blood group system.
1940	Drew receives a Doctor of Science in Surgery degree from Columbia University in June and returns to Howard University to teach.
1940–1941	Drew is medical supervisor of the Blood for Britain program from September 1, 1940, to January 1941.
1941	Drew is appointed assistant director of the Red Cross blood banks on February 3.
1944	Drew becomes Chief of Staff at Freedmen's Hospital.
1945	There are 600 African-American doctors in the armed forces by the end of World War II.
1947	The American Medical Association celebrates its 100th anniversary. It continues to refuse to admit Charles Drew and most black doctors. (The AMA finally integrates in 1968.)
1949	Drew is one of four doctors who tour military bases in Europe as consultants to the Surgeon General of the U.S. Army. There are more than 1,500 hospital blood banks in the United States, 46 nonhospital blood banks, and 31 American Red Cross regional blood centers.
1950	Plastic bags for blood collecting are introduced, replacing breakable glass bottles. Charles Drew dies on April 1.

RESOURCES

Bibliography

Harris, Marvin, *Our Kind: The Evolution of Human Life*. New York: Harper, 1989

Miller, Brandon Marie, *Just What the Doctor Ordered: The History of American Medicine*. Minneapolis: Lerner Publications Co., 1997

Myers, Walter Dean, *Now Is Your Time: The African-American Struggle for Freedom*. New York: Harper Collins, 1991

Myers, Walter Dean, *One More River to Cross*. New York: Harcourt Brace, 1995

Shapiro, Miles J., *Charles Drew: Life Saving Scientist*. Austin, TX: Steck-Vaughn Co., 1997

Wolfe, Rinna Evelyn, *Charles Richard Drew, MD*. New York: Franklin Watts, 1991

Web Sites

www. abcardio.org/body_charles_drew.htm: "Pioneering African American Doctors." Web site of the Association of Black Cardiologists, Inc.

www.howard.edu/huh-legacy/web3a.htm: Quiz about famous African-Americans. Web site of Howard University Hospital.

http://library.advanced.org/10329/Tourmenu.htm: Activities and games about African-Americans who have had postage stamps issued in their honor. Web site of the United States Post Office.

http://biomed.redcross/org/home/Dr-drew.htm: Web site of the American Red Cross.

http://www.pond.com/~pridgen/drew.htm: Web site of Drew's fraternity, Omega Psi Phi.

INDEX

Page numbers in italics refer to photographs.